MW00328112

God
Incidents

God Incidents

True Stories of God Working
in the Lives of Catholics

———◆———

Thomas R. Lukes

Foreword by Travis J. Vanden Heuvel
author of the bestselling book, *To Heaven & Back*

Nihil Obstat: Most Reverend Richard J. Garcia, D.D.
                 Bishop of the Diocese of Monterey

Scripture texts used in this book are taken from the *New American Bible*.
The Old Testament of the *New American Bible*, © 1970 by the Confraternity
of Christian Doctrine (CCD), Washington, D.C.; Revised New Testament
of the New American Bible © 1986 CCD. Used with permission.

English translation of the Catechism of the Catholic Church for the United
States of America, copyright 1994, United States Catholic Conference,
Inc.—Libreria Editrice Vaticana. English translation of the Catechism of
the Catholic Church: Modifications from the Editio Typica, copyright ©
1997, United States Conference, Inc.—Libreria Editrice Vaticana.

Every reasonable effort has been made to determine copyright holders of
excerpted materials and to secure permissions needed. If any copyrighted
materials have been inadvertently used in this work without proper credit
being given in one form or another, please notify the publisher in writing
so that future printings of this work may be corrected accordingly.

ISBN-13: 978-0-9993574-4-6
ISBN-10: 0999357446
Library of Congress Control Number: 2017909756

Cover design: Travis J. Vanden Heuvel
Cover photo © Peregrino Press 2018. ALL RIGHTS RESERVED
Printed in the United States of America

Peregrino Press, LLC
De Pere, WI
www.peregrino.press

This book is dedicated to our

Blessed Mother

Contents

Foreword

———•———

SUCCESS, AS DEFINED BY THE standards of the world in which we live, necessitates some rather monumental feats of juggling. Multi-tasking has been pushed to the limit, and keeping multiple balls in the air has become the new norm. Not only are we expected to work and parent and pursue personal improvement on multiple fronts, we're expected to do so with appropriate style and flair, utilizing gizmos and gadgets imbued with powers and capacities beyond our understanding.

What price, though, do we pay to keep up with the breakneck speed of life and to acquire the material objects necessary to be engaged with the world? In being pulled by the demands and rewards of work, do we give enough of ourselves to our families and loved ones? If devoting ourselves to family and loved ones results in failing to invest enough of ourselves in our jobs, are we willing to accept the cost and consequences accompanying such failure? And what will people think if we live without the newest smartphone, tech-integrated car, ultra-high definition television, or designer clothes?

In the context of this tug of war, what has become of our faith? For as busy as we keep ourselves, and for as connected as technology purports to make us, so many of us feel adrift. We get lost in a landscape offering infinite promise and possibility while ultimately failing to feed the yearning we all experience. We hunger for God and His presence in our lives, but we all feel abandoned by or cut off from Him at times. And in those times, we seek to fill the emptiness with other things – material, earthly things – only to find that they will never satisfy our spiritual hunger. This might even raise doubts about God's very presence in our lives and in our world.

We may, at the end of each day, feel alone.

But are we?

Our author assures us we are neither cut off nor abandoned, and in *God Incidents: True Stories of God Working in the Lives of Catholics*, Tom shares the stories of many people whose experiences bear witness to the immediate and unquestionably real presence of God in their lives. *God Incidents* resoundingly assures us that we are *not* alone.

With his background as an architect, Tom has always worked to create beauty and order. He has captured both in these stories. They open his readers' eyes to the design of a structure built by the greatest architect of them all, God Himself. God's Church may be visibly embodied in houses of worship, ranging from the simple church of the New Camaldoli Hermitage to the elaborate cathedrals we often envision, but the Church extends beyond brick and mortar, beyond altar and sacristy. God's Church is found, ultimately, in each of us. And if we believe that to be true, then we have a responsibility to share God with those around us; to be Christ to and for one another.

In the remarkable, true stories in *God Incidents*, we encounter abundant reminders that in our journey through this world, we are never alone. God is always with us and we may encounter His abundant love if we seek His presence by opening our minds and hearts. In these pages, you will read of Tom's own experiences, such as the challenge presented him as a confirmation instructor. But you'll also hear stories from other faithful Catholics – some ordinary, others extraordinary.

Margaret and Ray Tellez, for whom God provides all manner of blessings, find God through the sale of their family home in order to relocate closer to their daughter. Pete and Barbara Felice discover the truly profound healing power of their pilgrimage to Lourdes years after their visit. Kathleen Hicks, at a *silent* high school retreat, experiences the very volume and veracity of God's entreaty that in order to know Him she must love others: a profound lesson she carried forward into a life that combines vocation with avocation as she works daily with disabled children.

God Incidents, though, is only the beginning of Tom's effort to answer the call of our faith. Throughout his life, he has conditioned himself to seek God in the seemingly mundane and the ordinary. Through these stories, Tom offers ample evidence that God may, indeed, be found at any time, in any place. And just as God's love overflows for His creation, so do stories such as the ones you will find in this book. Tom, then, offers this volume as the foundation for an entire series of books that seeks to bring all of us closer to Christ.

Many of you are undoubtedly familiar with the popular *Chicken Soup for the Soul* series of books and the many variations it has inspired since its inception in the early nineties. These beloved books have been widely embraced by readers around the world for their ability to inspire and uplift. Similarly, *God Incidents* aims to inspire believers and seekers, the faithful and the skeptical, through stories of God's presence in the lives of the storytellers. The lived experiences of others, told in Tom's words, sketch a spiritual blueprint by which we come to recognize God's active involvement in all of our lives.

God Incidents is the beginning of something bigger than Tom, bigger than any one of us. Like so many of God's works made manifest in the world, they are brought to light in and through our brothers and sisters in Christ here on earth. Through their stories, we come to appreciate God's capacity to guide, direct, and inspire our thoughts, words, and deeds. In this manner, our works become His works; our words become His words; and our thoughts become His thoughts.

The key to any of this being so, however, hinges upon our recognition that His love for us is abundant and that His presence in our lives is real. For as different as all of the individuals and their stories may be in *God Incidents*, they are knit together by the common thread of God's true presence in our lives. It's my prayer that, through these stories – and the inspiration, contemplation, and examination they so naturally foster – we can recognize God's hand at work today, and all days.

Preface

MY JOURNEY IN WRITING THIS book all began one Friday morning when I picked up the October issue of *The Word Among Us*, which was devoted to *conversion*. The publisher, Joe Difato, shared with his readers what happened in 1971, when an event changed his life forever. It was only a one-page story, but I turned to my wife and told her that this is the type of story I really enjoy reading.

There is something about reading what God has done in people's lives that lifts my spirit. This is because reading this type of story shows God acting in people's lives. It makes God more real to me because what happens in the stories is so clearly *from God*. I find myself looking for stories like this to inspire me to be more faithful and prayerful. I often read books like this two or three times—each time with the same joy as the first time. Patrick Madrid's three-book series *Surprised by Truth* is a great example of this type of book.

I thought about all the events in my life that I call "God incidents." These are events that are beyond coincidence ("co-incidents"). They are religious experiences. They are either remarkable answers to prayer, conversions stories, or religious events that cannot be explained except by seeing God's hand in them.

I thought, why not write a book about a series of stories of God working in people lives? I could call it *God Incidents.* This could be an exciting and fulfilling project. I have had a number of experiences myself, ever since I made a Marriage Encounter—and later, Cursillo. But I realized that the impact of a collection of stories from different people would have a far greater impact than hearing stories from only one individual.

The more I thought about it, the more I liked the idea. The money raised from the book's sales could be donated to help support the parish schools in my diocese. This would result in a double blessing: the readers might see God as more real to them, and the profits from the book could help Catholic families give their children a life-changing education like the one I received as a youth. Also, I could incorporate scripture at the start of each chapter that would relate to the story. This would encourage reading the Bible and Bible study.

God's Direction

Saturday, I decided that I should pray about this idea for direction, so I prayed. I asked God for encouragement and direction that would show me if He really wanted me to write this book. Within two hours, I received a call from a friend from church. He asked me if I would take his place as lector to do the reading for the following day.

When I told him *yes*, I felt a nudge that this could be my answer, but my next thought was this: "Is God really going to give me a reading that says, 'Write this down?'" With this thought in my mind, I went into my study and got my lector's workbook down from the shelf and found the first reading for Sunday.

I discovered that it was from Habakkuk. The second paragraph began, *"Then the Lord answered me* and said: *Write down* the vision clearly upon the tablets, *so that one can read it readily"* (italics added for emphasis).

I just stood there in disbelief. God had given me a scripture that contained the words *write down!* The reading even said, "The Lord answered me..." and "...so that one can read it readily." I realized that I was not going to write down the stories on "tablets" but I got the gist of how to apply it to myself in my time. I could see that this was more than a coincidence, since it only appears on one Sunday every three years. This was the kind of *God incident* that I wanted to write about! God could not have made it clearer to me that this was His will.

How to Collect and Write the Stories

As soon as I thought more about writing this book, it soon

became clear that there would be many challenges ahead. I would need God's help, if I were to be successful. I realized that prayer and the Eucharist would need to keep me focused and strong to persevere through the journey. Many questions needed to be resolved.

Fr. Mike Miller of Sacred Heart Parish in Salinas, California, became my spiritual director. He encouraged me to use the names and parishes of the people in the Diocese of Monterey who shared their stories, once permission was obtained. Otherwise, if they didn't want me to use their full names, I could use a first name—or any first name they asked me to use. I started by writing down some stories that I had personally experienced, to develop some momentum and develop a format for the chapters.

The main difficulty in writing this book was not the actual writing but finding people who had stories to share and were willing to share them. I found that people who did not know me personally were reluctant to respond to a bulletin announcement to share stories. Although some did respond, I finally resorted to contacting people directly to tell them about the book, and to see if they had a story they were willing to share. A high percentage of these people did have stories to share.

Although people wanted to share their stories, they did not feel capable or skilled enough to write their story. For this reason, I chose to do the writing of all the stories. They were recorded on a Sony digital tape recorder, written by me, and then reviewed and approved by the original storyteller.

WHO ARE THE STORYTELLERS?

In Matthew Kelly's wonderful book *The Four Signs of a Dynamic Catholic*, Mr. Kelly shares that his research of many parishes in the United States revealed that "only 7.6% of Catholics are highly engaged." After deeper evaluation, he identifies this group as the "dynamic Catholics."

This is the same group of individuals who are fired up about their faith. These individuals are also those most likely to attend daily Mass. It was this group that I approached to share their stories. I also approached two priests, and both were willing to share a story.

Certainly God works in all of our lives, whether we are fired-up Catholics or not. However, I came to the conclusion that some people just may not be aware of, or even recognize that these actions are attributable to God. For me, sometimes it was well after the event that I was able to see God's hand in an earlier event in my life. I was not aware of it at the time. I was too distracted with raising a family and dealing with work to see God's action in my life.

FINAL THOUGHTS

I hope this book will make God more real to you and help you see God working in your and your family's lives. I also wrote these stories to allow you to feel comfortable sharing them with your children and your grandchildren, especially those who might be questioning if God even exists.

Enjoy!

Thomas R. Lukes

Introduction

IN THIS INTRODUCTION, I OFFER you a truly spiritual and transforming book that takes us on a blessed journey with our merciful God. These are journeys of deep faith. Thomas Lukes, the author of this book, interviewed many men and women, and he listened to their stories of God breaking into their lives. Just as Jesus called his Apostles to follow him, Thomas describes well the intimate and transforming stories of men and women who have had a special encounter with our loving God. *God Incidents* reminds us all that God desires with all his heart to accompany us on our journey toward God and to live with hope, joy, and love as we are called.

Our God is a God of love who also enjoys surprising us, as is so evident in the stories contained in this wonderful book of God's intervention in our lives. As I quote so often from the Acts of the Apostles, chapter 17, "God is never far from anyone of us." In these thirty-one stories, our brothers and sisters have felt and encountered God's closeness. Their stories invite us all to allow our loving God to break into our daily lives to encounter God and God's love for us.

May you and your families enjoy this wonderful spiritual work. Let us treasure it as God treasures us. Let us practice the presence of God in our lives.

+ *Richard J. Garcia*

+Most Reverend Richard J. Garcia, D.D.
Bishop of the Diocese of Monterey

CHAPTER 1

The Visions

———•———

Story from Paul Danielson, former Episcopal priest and parishioner at St. Joseph's Catholic Church in Spreckels, California

> *Jesus said to them, "Amen, amen, I say to you, unless you eat the flesh of the Son of Man and drink his blood, you do not have life within you. Whoever eats my flesh and drinks my blood has eternal life, and I will raise him on the last day."*

JOHN 6:53–54

TWENTY-FIVE MILES SOUTH OF BIG Sur on Highway 1 is the New Camaldoli Hermitage,[1] a monastery of Benedictine monks who offer a place for private retreat and prayer. The turn-off road to the monastery is immediately after Lucia and can be easily missed. In fact, unless you are looking for the sign next to the highway, you will miss it.

The road to the Hermitage climbs in hairpin turns up the mountainside for two miles, presenting great views of the rugged Pacific coastline, until finally, 1,300 feet above the ocean, you arrive in the parking lot of the bookstore and the Hermitage.

Since the Hermitage is a monastery where monks live in seclusion, it is not surprising that there is a six-foot-high wall that separates the entrance road and guest quarters from the monastery grounds where the monks live. Only family and special guests enter beyond the walls. The bookstore and the church are built along the wall, which permits the monks to serve the bookstore as well as participate in daily Mass where the public is welcome to attend. This interaction offers a glimpse of these men of prayer and contemplation.

The road continues past the bookstore another fifty yards to the guest quarters, which are perched on the hillside overlooking the Pacific and coastline below. There are eight single-unit motel-like accommodations, each with a private deck on the ocean side.

It was to this monastery that Paul Danielson chose to bring the vestry of Good Shepherd Episcopal Church for their annual *work weekend*. As pastor of a small church in the foothills between the cities of Salinas and Monterey, Paul felt that it was important for the key members of his staff and the newly elected members of the church council to get away for a long weekend each year. He saw it as a time to focus on the church's mission strategy for the upcoming year and to set goals, as well as a time for spiritual renewal. In a sense, it would be a *mini-retreat* for the vestry and their pastor.

Paul had heard great things about the New Camaldoli Hermitage from his parishioners, who had stayed at the guest accommodations, but he had never been there himself. When he called to make the arrangements, he learned that instead of the single-occupancy rooms at the guest quarters, the prior offered other accommodations where two or three could stay together—some down the hillside below the road and some within the walls of the monastery. The prior also promised a place where they could all eat together and meet for the planning that they hoped to accomplish for the next year.

When the vestry members arrived on Friday after work, they parked and were escorted to their rooms. After unpacking, Paul and the others gathered together for dinner. Greetings were shared among the group. There was a sense of anticipation in the air. The quiet and holiness of the place almost made them want to whisper. They couldn't help but wonder what this mysterious place might offer in the days ahead. They enjoyed a satisfying meal, while they discussed what was planned for the next day. Soon it was time to return to their rooms for the night.

On Saturday the vestry met and had lunch together, followed by free time for the afternoon. Some walked along the road, others just enjoyed the views out over the Pacific coast. It was a time to be by themselves for reflection, prayer, or sharing a moment with a friend. Paul was happy that they had chosen this place to spend the weekend together in work and contemplation. So it was that Saturday passed.

After breakfast on Sunday, the natural discussion turned to the Sunday church service. Since the prior had encouraged them to join the monks at Mass, everyone chose to gather in the church for the 11:00 a.m. Sunday Mass.

They had each explored the church during their free time. It was beautiful in its simplicity, but its layout was unlike any they had ever seen before. The church was composed of two distinct spaces: a small, low-ceiling, rectangular nave for seating attached to a hexagonal space where the altar was located.

The church is entered through a small vestibule that contains hymnals and other books on a large wood wall. Two openings flank the wood wall that separates the vestibule from the nave of the church. Upon moving past the vestibule, you find yourself in a small nave, where the pews do not face the length of the church but instead face the pews on the opposite side, with a twelve-foot aisle between them. It is here that the *Liturgy of the Word* takes place. At one end of this space is the priest's chair, which rests against the wood vestibule entrance wall, while the ambo (pulpit) is at the opposite end of the nave.

Beyond the ambo is a second, much larger space that is linked to the first by a large opening. Once inside this second space, you can see the great contrast to the nave. A granite altar rests in the center of a large room, hexagonal in shape, with its sloping roof meeting at a point high above. At the apex of the roof, where all the roof beams intersect, is a skylight from which hangs a silver crucifix. The altar is directly below the skylight and crucifix.

Two very wide steps surround the space on all sides and lead down to the level of the altar. It is here that the Liturgy of the Eucharist takes place.

In silent anticipation the vestry sat with about twenty others, waiting in the nave for the Mass to begin. Soon the monks entered from the left side of the nave, singing the "Entrance Antiphon" in a very beautiful Gregorian chant. They each wore white Benedictine-style robes. The celebrant wore vestments and proceeded to sit in the priest's chair at the end, facing the ambo and the altar beyond. The remainder of the monks divided themselves in the front row, on each side of the nave, in seats facing each other, with the assembly divided behind each side as the singing continued.

Paul described the feeling that "the Spirit there was real, clinging to the walls." The combination of the Gregorian chant and the simplicity of the church were captivating. One of the monks rose, walked to the ambo, and did the first reading. After a slight pause, another monk rose to lead the assembly in singing the Psalms in the same beautiful Gregorian chant. A long moment of silence followed. Then the celebrant rose and read the Gospel. Afterward, he returned to his chair to share his reflection of the readings. After the homily, everyone stood for the Nicene Creed, which was recited in a very deliberate and slow cadence that really made you think about what was being proclaimed.

After a pause, the monks rose, turned, and processed into the larger hexagonal space for *the Liturgy of the Eucharist.* Paul and the vestry members followed, as did the group from the other side of the church. Once inside the large space, the monks stationed themselves around the perimeter of the space at the lower level, while the assembly spaced themselves around the upper level against the outside concrete walls. The light from the skylight above focused the attention on the celebrant, who took his place as priest in front of the altar. The words of the *Consecration* had new meaning in that space.

> *Take this, all of you, and eat of it for this is my body,*
> *which will be given up for you.*

> *Take this all of you, and drink from it, for*
> *this is the chalice of my blood,*
> *which will be poured out for you and for*
> *many for the forgiveness of sins.*
> *Do this in memory of me.*

THE ROMAN MISSAL

When the priest raised the host in consecration, the monks all bowed in reverence together. Paul and the vestry members were so taken up with the beauty of the Mass that when it was time to receive communion, it seemed natural to join the rest of the congregation and fall in line behind the monks to receive Holy Communion. Paul received the Eucharist and returned, following the others, back to the pew.

As Paul sat with his eyes closed, simply sitting and being at peace with the Blessed Sacrament, he experienced a strange sensation. Although his eyes were closed, he realized that he was seeing a vision. "It was as if the walls of the church had melted away, and I saw the coastline and the Pacific stretched out to the horizon, but in the foreground was a huge figure of Our Lord moving toward me with hands outstretched with love in his eyes and light surrounding him." No words were spoken, but Paul said his sense was one of welcome and love. Paul sat absorbed in silent wonder for some time. Finally, the concluding prayers of the Mass brought Paul back to reality.

After the Mass, the vestry shared lunch together before returning to their quarters to pack up and head home to Salinas and Monterey. While others spoke of the holiness of the place, Paul chose not to share his experience, since he was afraid others might question it. He was also still reveling in the sensation of seeing the figure of Christ that was so real to him. He did not want to let anyone spoil it.

Judging from everyone's comments, it was clear to Paul that the weekend retreat had been a great success. Soon they returned to their rooms. Paul would be traveling home with two vestry members, Frank and Vic. At first the three of them rode in silence, each absorbed in his own thoughts and the enchanting beauty of the coastline that stretched out in front of them.

After some time, Vic broke the silence, saying, "I have to tell you about what I experienced today at Mass. After I went to communion, I returned to my seat and closed my eyes like I always do. Except this time, something strange happened. I saw a vision of Christ with his hands outstretched toward me." Paul said that Vic then went on to describe in exact detail the very same vision that he had experienced.

It was not until years later at the Easter vigil Mass in 2005 that Paul responded to the outstretched hands of Christ when he was welcomed into the Catholic Church. (Paul died of cancer March 1, 2016 at 77. He is greatly missed.)

---

[1] The New Camaldoli Hermitage is a rural Camaldolese Benedictine hermitage in the Santa Lucia Mountains of Big Sur, California, in the United States. The Camaldolese branch of the Benedictine family was founded by St. Romuald in the late tenth century. The hermitage was founded in 1958 by two monks from the motherhouse in Camaldoli in northern Italy.

CHAPTER 2

Dreams

———◆———

Story from Will Souza from St. Joseph's Catholic Church in Spreckels, California

> *I am the good shepherd. I know mine and mine know me,*
> *just as the Father knows me and I know the Father; I will*
> *lay done my life for the sheep. I have other sheep that do*
> *not belong to this fold. These also I must lead, and they will*
> *hear my voice, and there will be one flock, one shepherd.*

JOHN 10:14–16

WILL SAT IN THE DARKNESS of his bedroom, thinking. He was still half asleep. It was so real! He could still see the body and feel the fear. He had to tell himself that it was just a dream. The images came back again. He had been standing in a bare room—but not by himself. There were two other figures with him. On a slab-like table in front of him lay the body of a young man whom he did not recognize, while at the other end of the table stood Satan, evil and menacing.

9

In the dream, Will and the devil were arguing over the body. Finally, Will said, "I claim him in the name of Jesus." Then, he reached out and touched the body, which immediately disappeared in a bright flash. The flash woke Will, but the fear remained. He just sat on his bed, thinking. What did this dream mean? It had been so real and frightening. Who was the dead person that he was claiming for Christ?

The phone rang. Will learned that Jimmy, his confirmation godson had been killed that night in a car accident. As Will hung up the phone in sorrow and disbelief, his thoughts immediately returned to his dream. Will immediately knew that the body was Jimmy.

He now had to decide if he should share his dream with Jimmy's mom and dad. He knew that Jimmy was one of seven children. His father was a dairy farmer. Will thought about what they must be going through, dealing with the death of their son. Will wasn't sure what to do. He asked God if he should tell the parents about his dream. God said, "Yes!"

Later in the day, Will called Jimmy's home and spoke to Jimmy's mother, Ann. Will told her of his dream on the night of the accident. His story seemed to lift her from her grief. She thanked Will for sharing his dream. She told Will what had happened to her on the night of the accident.

Ann had gone to bed after Jimmy left to go out with two of his high school friends. She was awakened by a very disturbing dream of her own that involved three lambs. The impact of the dream was so terrifying that she got out of bed, put on her robe, and started praying for the three young men. She was still pacing the floor when the phone's ring startled her. She learned that her son was dead, killed by a car that had run a stop sign in the fog. The other boys were unhurt. After relating her dream, Ann thanked Will over and over again for sharing his dream with her.

CHAPTER 3

The Hitchhiker

Story from Fr. Michael Miller, pastor of Sacred Heart Catholic Church in Salinas, California

> *[Jesus] said to them again, "Peace be with you. As the Father has sent me, so I send you." And when he had said this, he breathed on them and said to them, "Receive the Holy Spirit. Whose sins you forgive are forgiven them, and whose sins you retain are retained."*
>
> *JOHN 20:21–23*

"THIS IS A STORY OF how, when you are beginning something, and you are just not sure if it is right or not, sometimes God will give you a sign to move ahead." (Fr. Mike Miller)

About three years after becoming a priest during the late 1970s, Fr. Mike Miller continued his studies at the Graduate Theological Union at Berkeley. On weekends, he served as an associate at St. David's Catholic Church in the nearby city of Richmond.

Once the quarter was completed, Fr. Mike began to plan for his one-month vacation from his duties at St. David's. He wanted to get out of the big-city rush, do some traveling, and find some solitude. This would give him time for reflection on what had been happening in his life as a student and young priest.

With time on his hands and a longing to get away, Fr. Mike had one major problem: he had very little money to spend on going anywhere by train or plane, and he didn't own a car, so he followed the example of many of his fellow students. He decided to try *hitchhiking*.

In Berkeley there was a favorite spot for students to hitchhike near the campus. In that university town, it was common to see students standing beside their backpacks and holding a sign, while extending their thumbs in the universal sign of the hitchhiker.

Fr. Mike decided to arrive before other students showed up, hoping to get an early start. This way he might be able to get a ride before he was just part of the throng of younger students waiting with him.

Fr. Mike set down his backpack, and as each potential ride approached, he held up his sign that read simply, "NORTH OR EAST." He felt secure that no one would know that he was a priest, since he looked like any other college student.

Soon it was clear that the early-morning start wasn't going to help. As time went by, and no one stopped, he was soon joined by other students, until finally at least fourteen others had parked themselves in front of him.

He was just getting to the point of quitting for the day when a car slowed and turned toward the group of hitchhikers. The car slowed down to a crawl...and then moved down the group of hitchhikers, clearly checking them out. When it stopped in front of Fr. Mike, he was a little apprehensive about getting in, but he realized that trusting people had become part of his role as a priest. Trust was essential if he was to minister to God's children.

Fr. Mike opened the door and felt all apprehension leave him when he saw that the driver looked like an average guy in his mid-thirties. The driver said his name was Jeff. He was going as far as Reno, so Fr. Mike hopped in without the slightest thought of what God might have in store for him on the ride ahead.

Although the driver introduced himself as Jeff, Fr. Mike didn't want him to know he was a priest, so he told Jeff his name was just Mike, rather than Fr. Mike. He soon learned that Jeff was a vice squad policeman from San Francisco. He was just looking for someone to keep him company on his four-hour trip to Reno.

Jeff's talk at first was just small talk, but it wasn't long until his tone changed, and he got more serious. "Do you want to hear something weird?" he asked. "Sure," Fr. Mike responded.

Jeff continued, "I was born Catholic. That probably means nothing to you, but when you are born and raised Catholic, sometimes it gets in your blood, and you can't get rid of it. I left the church when I got out of high school. I just thought it was a bunch of baloney. But lately, I've wanted to go back. I have gone to Mass a few times, but I just can't get up enough nerve to talk to a priest to go to confession."

Fr. Mike was not sure what to say. He was afraid to tell Jeff he was a priest. He was afraid Jeff would think that he was making fun of him, since he was so much younger than Jeff. He also didn't think Jeff would believe him, but he soon found an opportunity as they passed through Richmond. "We just passed St. David's Catholic Church where I work," he said.

Jeff responded, "Oh, are you the janitor?"

Fr. Mike smiled and said, "Oh, you probably won't believe me, but I am a priest there."

Jeff turned and took a long look at the young man he had picked up. The gaze was one of surprise mixed with a look of scrutiny. Fr. Mike only wished he had some proof on him to show that he was indeed a priest, but he knew he had brought nothing that would help.

Their friendly discussion continued until two hours later, as the highway started the rise into the mountains. There was a long pause. Jeff turned to Fr. Mike and said, "Would it be all right if I pulled off the freeway, so you could hear my confession?"

Fr. Mike said, "Oh that would be wonderful!"

So in the foothills of the Sierras, Fr. Mike acting in *persona Christi*, heard Jeff's confession—beginning Jeff's return to the Catholic Church of his youth.

Much later, as Fr. Mike lay in his sleeping bag under the clear, star-filled Nevada sky, he couldn't help but marvel at what had taken place that day. Was it by chance that Jeff had picked him out of all the hitchhikers on the street in Berkeley? Did God ordain that in their short time together so much would happen? God had both eased Jeff back into the church and showed Fr. Mike that God would use him to reach His children.

Only the rustle of the wind through the leaves broke the silence. In his heart Fr. Mike knew that he had no fear of the journey ahead of him. The Spirit of God was with him.

CHAPTER 4

A Precious Child

Story from Jaime and Kati from St. Joseph's Catholic Church
in Spreckels, California

> *Blessed be God, the Father of our Lord Jesus Christ, the*
> *Father of compassion and God of all encouragement, who*
> *encourages us in our every affliction, so that we may be*
> *able to encourage those who are in any affliction with the*
> *encouragement with which we ourselves are encouraged by God.*

2 CORINTHIANS 1: 3–4

SOBBING, JAIME SAT INDIAN-STYLE AT the end of her bed
with Kati, her one-week old child, raised over her head.
Looking up toward heaven, she cried out to God, "If you have
to take her, I give her to you. But if this is what you want, you
will have to help me get through this."

Jaime's first pregnancy with her son, Cooper, had been un-
eventful, but this second pregnancy with Kati had been

difficult. Those memories were set aside with the sight of Jaime's beautiful little baby. It was not until Kati was five days old that the doctor broke the news that little Kati had a serious heart condition. She would require open heart surgery at six weeks. Jaime and her husband, Paul, were told the frightening prognosis: Kati had only a fifty-fifty chance of surviving the surgery. Fear came over Jaime. She thought, "I might lose my child!" This had led her to cry out to God for help.

Paul and Jaime, and their families and friends, all prayed for a successful surgery. Prayer helped calm their anxiety, but it was not enough to totally overcome their fear. As Jaime said, "We lived in fear every day up to the surgery."

During the surgery, their prayers flooded heaven with heart-felt intensity like no other time in Jaime's or Paul's life. Time seemed to pause as the anxiety mounted. The hours passed, but there was still no word. Finally, Kati's doctor came out to speak with them. They could see by the smile on his face that he had good news. Everything had gone well. They were overjoyed!

Later at the doctor's office, he explained to Jaime and Paul what was in store for Katie in the years ahead. They learned that when Kati had passed her growth spurt as an early teen-ager, she would require another surgery to replace the heart valve. This meant that in the back of their minds there would be another event that they must face: *another open heart surgery.*

Once a year, Jaime took Kati to the doctor for her annual checkup. As Kati grew old enough to understand, her parents explained that she was born with a heart condition, but they avoided telling her about the future surgery. They decided to wait until later; otherwise, she might live in fear of that day.

When Kati was fourteen, the doctor said it was time for the surgery. Jaime's thoughts flashed back to years earlier, when she had lifted little Kati to God. Jaime felt that same fear again, but she realized that she had trusted God then. Now she had to trust Him again. Kati was in God's hands. When Jaime asked the doctor about the survival rate, he said there was very little risk with this second surgery, so Jaime and Paul tried not to worry.

When the day of the surgery arrived, Jaime and Paul prayed for a successful surgery. Again the doctor had good news; the surgery had gone well. Kati had received a bioidentical valve that would need to be replaced in five to ten years. It meant yet another surgery ahead. But with each successful surgery, they had built up a trust in Kati's doctor and in God.

As much as they didn't want to think about another heart surgery for Kati, the doctor always reminded them of this at Kati's annual exam. The doctor always said that Kati was progressing well, but each visit brought them closer to another surgery.

When Kati was a freshman in high school, there was a new reason for a visit to her doctor. Kati wanted to ride on the mountain bike team for Salinas High School. She needed to receive permission from her doctor. She underwent a stress test that went well, and she was given permission. Again, the doctor adjusted the surgery date by one year (three to eight years away). The surgery date was growing closer.

By this time, Jaime had been working at St. Joseph's parish office in Spreckels three days a week. This made it possible for her to get out of the house and to contribute to the family income. She liked it there. Everyone was friendly and she had quickly made new friends.

One morning Donna Doss, the office manager, brought a letter to Jaime. "Read over this and see what you think." The letter was from Patrick Kraft, a parishioner at Carmel Mission and a Knight of the Order of Malta.[1] The letter had been sent to all the parishes in the Diocese of Monterey. It was about a pilgrimage to Lourdes offered to those sick who could qualify.

The Knights' pilgrimage to Lourdes is limited to fifty sick individuals from the western states. To qualify for the pilgrimage, you must go through a selection process. This is what Patrick Kraft's letter addressed. Donna wanted to nominate Kati for this pilgrimage, since she appeared to meet the criteria, which included the following:

ꝝ The candidate must be suffering from a serious health issue.

ꝝ The candidate could not be on oxygen.

ꝝ The candidate must be ambulatory, or his or her companion must be able to take care of him or her.

If accepted, Kati's entire expenses for the trip would be paid, and Jaime would be allowed to come along as her "companion," paying her own way. Fr. Roy Shelly, the pastor at St. Joseph Catholic Church, thought it was a great idea. He offered to nominate Kati as the parish's candidate to the Order of Malta.

Jami thought this was a great opportunity to see Lourdes and to get help for Kati through the famous healing waters.

Everything moved quickly from that time forward: Fr. Roy wrote the letter nominating Kati; Kati's doctor wrote the patient evaluation; and finally, both Jaime and Kati wrote their required letters. The final requirement in the process was an interview with a Dame of Malta, who as an MD could best evaluate both the *malade* (Kati) and her *companion* (Jaime).

The interview with a Dame of Malta didn't seem to bother the seventeen-year-old Kati. "All I could think about during the interview was the Forty-Niner's game that the family was going to afterward." The interview went well.

Finally, the notification came to the office that Kati had been selected for the pilgrimage to Lourdes. This left Jaime six weeks to obtain a passport for Kati and get ready for the trip. They flew from San Jose to Los Angeles, where they joined up with about two hundred others from the western region to travel by charter directly to Lourdes.

When they arrived in Lourdes at 11:00 a.m., they immediately went out to look around. Jaime recounted, "We had to buy croissants and sit by the river to take in the architecture and listen to the language." There was much to take in and so many pilgrims, most of them with the Order of Malta from other areas of the United States and Europe. More than twenty-five thousand pilgrims with the Order of Malta were at Lourdes that week from all over the world.

The nine-hour time difference and the eleven-hour flight took their toll on Jaime and Kati. Sleep came easily that first night, but the morning brought disappointment. Jaime woke up incredibly sick. Not only was she sick physically, but she was emotionally upset that her first full day at Lourdes would be spent in her room. She so desperately wanted to be out with Kati and the others, especially because this was the day that the *malades* were to go into the baths.

Soon, a knight and dame of Malta arrived to take Kati to the events planned for the day. Seeing Kati's departure and realizing that she was too sick to join Kati became unbearable for Jaime. Crying and upset with the turn of events, she cried out to God, "Why, why am I even here?" Jaime received this loud response, "God needs you out of His way to work through Kati."

Jaime immediately stopped crying and started laughing. She said, "It totally made sense, because I'm one of those moms—I'm not a *helicopter mom*, but I do tend to keep an eye on my daughter." This was just the first part of the message. The second part was, "You need to let her go." Jaime knew immediately that this referred to the first days of Kati's life, when Jaime gave Kati to the Lord, lifting her up to God. Jaime needed to again release Kati into God's care. She realized that this was not about death; it was about allowing Kati to grow up—to bloom and become the young woman that God wanted her to be without her mom's hovering.

While Jaime lay sick back at the hotel, Kati was having a great time exploring Lourdes with the Malta group. After lunch, Kati waited in line with other women on the pilgrimage to go into the baths[2] to experience the healing water[3] of Lourdes.

When it was Kati's turn to enter the bath area, she discovered that there were two French ladies helping direct her into the changing room and assisting her into the bath. She quickly slipped off her clothes, and they helped her put on a wet blue wrap.

The bath was approximately 4' x 8' x 30" deep rectangular recess in concrete floor. It was half-filled with clear water. The bath is entered from one end down concrete steps. A square, colored, plate-like ceramic frieze of the head of Blessed Mother looked down on Kati as she approached the bath. At the direction of one of the French ladies, she made the sign of the cross before she stepped into the water.

Later, Kati reported to her mom, "When my toes first touched the water, something happened! I felt a hand on my shoulder. I felt a tingling from my head to my toes. I felt Mary's presence throughout the experience." Overwhelmed by the coldness of the water, Kati was anxious to just "cleanse her body" with splashes of water rather than to sit down in the bath. When she got out to dry off, she discovered that she was already completely dry! Others had told her that this might happen, but she didn't believe it until she had experienced it herself.

The next morning, Jaime was finally able to get outside, having completely recovered from being so sick. Mom and daughter spent the remainder of their trip with different knights and dames, attending daily Mass and visiting the sights of Lourdes, which included visiting the grotto, seeing Bernadette's family church, and seeing the house where Bernadette and her family lived—an abandoned jail. After the eight-day trip was over, they returned home with more than three thousand photographs and many great memories.

Two weeks after arriving home, they went to see Kati's doctor for her annual check-up visit. Jaime and Kati were accustomed to the series of tests that Kati had to undergo. They consisted of an EKG, an echocardiogram, followed by the doctor's methodical listening to Kati's heart with his stethoscope. It had all become a routine for them—except this time something was different.

After the exam, the doctor put his hands in his white doctor's coat pockets, and with a puzzled look, he paused momentarily in thought and then said, "Your body has adapted so well to the valve, it will be decades before it needs replacing. In fact, if there were a hundred patients who had had the same operation, maybe one of them would have had this result." Jaime was stunned!

It was not until they got back in the car that Jaime discovered that Kati did not really understand the significance of what the doctor had just announced. Once she explained it to Kati, they both broke down and cried together.

Kati asked through her sobs, "Do you think it is from Lourdes?"

Her mom asked back, "What do you think?"

Kati responded, "I think it was."

---

[1] The Order of Malta was originally a military order of lay people founded around the year 1050 to provide protection for pilgrims, as well as to care for the poor and sick traveling to the Holy Land. Today, the Order of Malta still provides care of the poor and sick, but now they are not limited to helping those in the Holy Land. The Order of Malta includes more than thirteen thousand knights and dames; eighty thousand permanent volunteers; and twenty thousand medical personnel, including doctors, nurses, and paramedics, in more than 120 countries. California is part of the western region of the Order of Malta. Its main focus each year is to lead a pilgrimage to bring the sick to the healing waters of Lourdes in southern France. (Source: Wikipedia)

[2] "The current baths were constructed in 1955 and upgraded in 1972 and 1980. There are seventeen separate bath cubicles—eleven for women and six for men. Each year, about 350,000 people visit the baths." (Source: Wikipedia).

[3] The water is from the same spring that Bernadette, on February 24, 1858, uncovered at Mary's direction in the grotto of Lourdes during the ninth apparition. The instructions of Our Lady were to "drink at the spring and bathe in it." There had not been a spring there until Bernadette had started digging in the sand. Today, this spring has provided healing for hundreds of sick people, since the first two-year-old boy, near death, was cured of tuberculosis in 1858. (There have been sixty-seven official cures approved by the Church.)

CHAPTER 5

Ruth

———•———

Story from Dr. Robert Keaney from Carmel Mission in
Carmel by the Sea, California

> *Grant, Lord God, that we, your servants, may rejoice in*
> *unfailing health of mind and body, and, through the glorious*
> *intercession of Blessed Mary ever-virgin, may we be set free from*
> *present sorrow and come to enjoy eternal happiness. Through*
> *our Lord Jesus Christ, your Son, who lives and reigns with you*
> *in the unity of the Holy Spirit, one God, for ever and ever.*
>
> COLLECT FROM THE ROMAN MISSAL ON *5-30-15*

B OB'S PARENTS, JIM AND RUTH Keaney, were Irish
Catholics who lived with their four children in Providence,
Rhode Island. Jim was a mailman, and Ruth had the responsi-
bility of raising their children, Jackie, Jim, Bob, and Maureen.

Bob's story really begins when his father died of a heart attack.
Bob was just nine. This brought about a major crisis in the

family. Not only had Ruth lost her husband and the children lost their father, but Ruth was faced with the huge challenge of raising four children, ages four to thirteen, while surviving only on her husband's pension from the US Postal Service.

Back in the 1950s, there was no daycare or preschool to allow Ruth to work while the kids were in someone's care. Indeed, the thought of leaving her young ones in the care of a stranger was not likely something that Ruth would have considered. The option that Ruth chose was to trust in God to get them through these years. It meant sacrifice, and often doing without builds character. Bob said, "We grew up with nothing." He said this not as an adult who was looking back with regret but just as a matter-of-fact statement of how it was.

Ruth must have been a strong Catholic, because her trust in God's providence was important during this challenging time. Bob said that her biggest concern was to make sure her children received a Catholic education. Initially, the older children went to the parish elementary school. Later, Jackie, the oldest, attended high school, but when Jim was ready for high school, a new family crisis developed. Ruth did not have the money necessary to send both children to the Catholic high school, which cost $100 to $200 per child per year. She realized that even if she could come up with Jackie's and Jim's tuition, what would she do when her other children were ready for high school?

This did not stop Ruth. She went to her pastor and told the

monsignor the situation. His response was simple and loving. "I will make a deal with you. If you teach catechism to the public school kids twice a week, I will pay the tuition." Even though Ruth had no training in teaching, she did know her catechism, so she readily agreed to the arrangement.

Ruth also received help from her own children to contribute money to support the family. When they turned sixteen, Ruth had them meet with a close friend of her husband, who was the general manager of a large supermarket chain. He put them to work after school and on weekends. The jobs were union jobs, so they were well paid. The money they earned went into the family bowl on the kitchen table to help Ruth meet the family expenses, which were growing as the children started high school and were eating more food and requiring more expensive clothes than when they were little.

The effect of the pastor's decision to help Ruth send her four children to Catholic high schools was profound. The girls attended St. Francis Xavier School for Girls, while Bob and Jim attended Bishop Hendricken High School. Hendricken was an all-male college-preparatory high school taught by the Brothers of the Holy Cross. "Hendricken was an exceptional school," Bob recalls.

At Hendricken, Jim and Bob were challenged with hours of homework and exams all the time. Sometimes, they would have to study all night. It was there that the brothers learned how to study. They received an excellent education. Bob said that they both felt they learned more at Hendricken than they did at either Yale or Brown University, where they attended college. Both went on to become doctors of medicine.

Bob presently works at Community Hospital of the Monterey Peninsula as an emergency physician, while Jim also is an emergency physician but in the San Francisco Bay area. Maureen became an attorney after graduating from Providence College and Villanova. Bob's oldest sister, Jackie, even though Ruth called her the brightest of the four children, chose to marry and be a mom.

After the four children graduated from high school, Ruth worked for twenty years in a silver business, the owner of which was also a friend of the family. When Ruth applied for the job, she had to fill out an application with many questions, some of which were to be answered by checking a *Yes* or *No* box. Perhaps Ruth was a little nervous about applying for her first job. This might explain what happened. After she turned in the application, the owner came to her and said, "We have a slight problem here." Ruth had checked a box that indicated she was a convicted felon. After clearing up this mistake, Ruth started her first-ever job, which she held until she retired some twenty years later.

Ruth attended daily Mass the last ten years of her life. She had a real Marian devotion. In fact, Bob's early memory of his mom at church always included an image of Ruth holding a Rosary in her hand.

Bob and Jim had tried to persuade their mom to move out to California to be with them—but without success. It wasn't until Ruth's brother and sister died that Ruth was willing to leave her home in Rhode Island and join her sons in California. Maureen helped her move out and decided to stay, while Jackie remained in Rhode Island to raise her family.

In her later years, Ruth suffered from diabetes and was forced to use a walker. Maureen took care of Ruth during the last three years of her life. In 1994, when she was in her seventies, Ruth died at Stanford hospital while recovering from heart surgery.

Bob described his mom as "the glue of the family" and "the best mother in the world," so it is understandable that Ruth's four children took her death hard. It was about two months after her death that Bob had the first dream. "The most vivid-real dream I have ever had. There is my mother in heaven, standing with Mary—the same size and shape, dressed identically. Both had veils and were dressed in Carolina blue and white... like you typically see Mary wearing, arm in arm, shoulder to shoulder, barefoot, both of them identically dressed. My mom turns to me, puts her hand up to her mouth like she wants to share a little secret, and whispers, '*I love it up here!*' And that was the end of the dream."

Knowing Ruth was very devoted to Mary, Bob said that to see them as buddies gave him a sense of reassurance. Within a month Bob had the second dream of his mom and Mary together again. This time, Ruth and Mary were sitting in the front car of a rollercoaster beginning to head down from the highest point. They were again dressed alike, but this time, each held on to the other's head covering with one hand, while the other hand was raised high. Both had an expression of pure glee on their faces.

There was no question in Bob's mind: Ruth was enjoying being in heaven…a lot!!

CHAPTER 6

Hands of Fire

———◆———

Story from Tom Lukes from St. Joseph's Catholic Church in Spreckels, California, and Sacred Heart Army Chapel in Seaside, California

> *When the apostles in Jerusalem heard that Samaria had accepted the word of God, they sent them Peter and John, who went down and prayed for them that they might receive the Holy Spirit, for it had not yet fallen upon any of them; they had only been baptized in the name of the Lord Jesus. Then they laid hands on them and they received the Holy Spirit.*

ACTS 8:14–17

LOCATED IN MONTEREY, SAN CARLOS Borromeo is the cathedral church of the Monterey Diocese. It was completed by the Franciscan Father Junípero Serra as the chapel of Carmel Mission on June 3, 1770.

I have always loved the beauty of this church, especially the beautiful paintings of the Stations of the Cross and the realistic figure of Christ nailed to the round wooden members of the cross. This is the most beautiful crucifix I have ever seen. You can almost feel the pain that Christ endured for mankind.

San Carlos Cathedral is only a twenty-minute drive from my home in the oak-covered hills outside of Salinas. It was the Tuesday night prayer meeting that encouraged me to drive to San Carlos Cathedral this particular night.

The *Prayer Meeting* always began with music and singing that was not only beautiful but rich in meaning. The songs spoke to me deeply. You could sense that we were in the presence of God. This was further underscored by the gold tabernacle where I knew Jesus was present in the Blessed Sacrament.

I was amazed at the spirit that filled the gathering. The singing and music really affected me. In fact, the chorus of one song kept going through my head that night on the way home and throughout the night. Even when I would awaken, the chorus continued, almost as if music were playing above me in my bedroom.

"Lord I Lift Your Name on High"

You came from heaven to earth, to show the way.
From the earth to the cross, my debt to pay.
From the cross to the grave, from the grave to the sky, Lord,
I lift your name on high.

RICK DOYLE FOUNDS

Several weeks passed before I again felt the urge to head off to Monterey after dinner and become part of that spirit of praising God. When the music and praise portion of the meeting ended, the group leader, Michael Haggerty, invited anyone who wished to come forward to be *prayed over* for whatever need they had—This was something different from my last visit.

I thought that I would just wait and watch as some people went forward to be prayed over. I had an urging to go forward, but I thought: I was not sick, I didn't need prayer for anything, and my family was fine. But something inside me needed prayer. So finally I decided I would go up and ask to be prayed over "to have more joy in my life."

As I walked up to the altar area, I realized that I had waited too long, because by this time, all members of the prayer team were each praying over someone. But since I had walked forward, I decided that I would just wait until someone was finished, so they could pray over me.

Pairs of people were gathered around the altar area, receiving prayer. So I stood there behind the altar to wait my turn. I was standing looking up at the crucifix that was so real and powerful.

I turned around and looked back over the altar down the main aisle of this old church and waited. About this time, I noticed that an older woman had just collapsed. She had been prayed over not more than six feet away from me. Fortunately, she had been caught by the outstretched arms of a team member. She seemed to be resting at complete peace on the tile floor behind the altar. This was not exactly what I had in mind when I came up there to be prayed over. I thought what if this happens to me?

Then, I noticed a young man coming up the aisle. I was sure that he must be coming to be prayed over as well. He came right toward me, and I expected him to wait beside me. But instead, he asked me if I was there to be prayed over. When I said *yes*, he then asked me what it was that I wanted to be prayed over for. "To have more joy in my life," I replied. It was not until he asked me to turn to face the crucifix that I realized that he intended to pray over me!

He put his hands on my head and began praying silently, while I stood and faced him and the wall that held the tabernacle and body of Christ on the Cross. After he had prayed for some time, he stopped and asked me if I had been reading the Bible. I was just starting to answer him, when I felt hands come to rest on my back. *They were on fire!* I stopped mid-sentence, unable to continue. I wanted to tell him that it was all right...I didn't need to answer his question... that my prayer was being answered. I was filled with *joy* to such a degree that I could only say *yes* to him.

As he began to pray again, I continued to experience a great joy that took my breath away. When finally the praying ended, I turned to see who was behind me, and I discovered that it was Bob Cuva, the leader of the prayer group, who had not been there during the Prayer Meeting but who must have arrived late to help out with the praying.

I still could not talk. I simply shook their hands and headed home. The feeling of joy continued for the twenty-minute ride home. My family was all asleep, but even as I got into bed, the joy continued.

God has never been more real to me than He was that night when *hands of fire* surprised me with God's gift of *joy!*

CHAPTER 7

Guardian Angel

Story from Stephen Lukes from St. Joseph's Catholic Church in Spreckels, California

In just the same way, it is not the will of your heavenly Father that one of these little ones be lost.

MATTHEW 18:14

EVERY MORNING WHEN I WOULD leave for work, I would ask God to protect my family, especially my two young sons. It just seemed that when I was away, anything could happen to my young boys, who were just one and three years old. This attitude continued for as long as I can remember. Then, about ten years later, when Stephen was born, I found my protective love for Stephen no different. I really believe God gives fathers this protective love—a "lay down your life" kind of love.

When Stephen was about eight or ten, he and two friends took their bikes and rode over to a development of homes behind us, where there were new areas to explore and hills to ride down. Everything went fine until Stephen headed down the asphalt roadway. The faster he went, the more his handlebars began to shake—until he couldn't stop them from turning. In an instant, he lost control, the wheel turned at right angles to the road, and he went flying over the handlebars.

Stephen landed on his head on the asphalt and tumbled down the roadway. Unfortunately, he was not wearing a helmet. His friends rushed to see if he was all right, only to see Stephen get up with only a scrape on his knee.

His first words were, "Did you see her?" They both looked at Stephen, puzzled. When he related this story to his mother, Stephen explained that he had seen a lady all in white, who had cradled his head in her arms during his fall.

Stephen's scraped-up knee was the only sign that he had been in a serious bike accident. Landing on his head, going as fast as he was going, could have ended his life or left him paralyzed had it not been for his heavenly protector.

We never were sure if the lady in white was his guardian angel or our Blessed Mother looking after our child. Looking back on this event, it reminded me of my many prayers for the protection of my children. God does answer our prayers! We can never fully comprehend His love for us.

CHAPTER 8

Listening

Story from Ray Souza from St. Joseph's Catholic Church in
Spreckels, California

> *There are different kinds of spiritual gifts but the same*
> *Spirit; there are different forms of service but the same*
> *Lord; there are different workings but the same God who*
> *produces all of them in everyone. To each individual the*
> *manifestation of the Spirit is given for some benefit.*

1 CORINTHIANS 12:4–7

RAY HAD PARTICIPATED IN ST. Joseph's RENEW program mainly because many of his friends had signed up,
and perhaps more importantly, his wife Pam wanted to be part
of it too. They were involved for twelve to eighteen months.
After the experience, Ray had to admit that he enjoyed the
interaction and faith sharing. In fact, Ray said that his experience in RENEW "opened a few doors and unclouded a
few windows for me." So when a fellow member of his group

mentioned that he had noticed a change in Ray over the time together, Ray joked, "I'm getting so bad, I'm going to make Cursillo one of these days."

Before RENEW was popular in the Diocese of Monterey, Cursillo was the most popular form of renewal that was offered in the diocese. Cursillo began in 1962 in California, and it continues to this day. Once Ray experienced RENEW, it is understandable that he would consider Cursillo. Some years earlier, the Simmons had invited Ray and Pam to attend a Cursillo. Back then, Ray had no desire to go on a Cursillo, but after his Renew experience, he actually felt that he was ready.

In the 1990s, Cursillo Weekends were put on in the spring and fall of the year. Ray realized one was coming up the following month, so he contacted Judge Simmons and his wife, Antoinette, and asked them if they would still be willing to sponsor Ray and his wife on the upcoming Weekend. The Simmons were delighted that Ray and Pam finally wanted to go, and they quickly supplied applications for the upcoming Weekend.

Ray shared that the talk that stuck with him the most on the Cursillo was the one given by Gene Cunningham, "a big guy who was a contractor from Monterey." Ray still remembers Gene saying how difficult it was for him when he came home from the Cursillo to tell his wife that she was no longer number one in his life. Now God had that spot. This really had an impact on Ray.

That night on the Cursillo, Ray couldn't sleep, so he slipped out of the dorm and walked down to the chapel for a little quiet time with God. The only light in the chapel was the red tabernacle light, which announced to all that Jesus was present in the tabernacle in the Blessed Sacrament.

For a while, Ray just sat there and thought about what he had experienced on the first day of the Cursillo. Then what Gene had said came back to him. "It dawned on me that what Gene had said was absolutely right." Ray had not just put Pam before God in his life but many other things too. "God may not have even been in the top ten in my life at that time." Ray knew this would change as a result of the Cursillo.

Ray approached the tabernacle and lovingly put a hand on each side of it. "The coolness of the metal could not overcome the feeling of warmth that penetrated its sides." Ray was at peace in the darkness of the chapel. This moment was the highlight of Ray's Cursillo Weekend.

Years had passed since his Cursillo, but the experience still affected him. He still tried to put God first in his life, and perhaps because of this, Ray had developed a special relationship with God. He had become more aware of God's will in his life. He shared several examples:

Ray's father was a dairy farmer, and because of this he had always impressed Ray by his fortitude and drive. "He was strong as an ox, especially in his upper body." He was a hard worker who also worked long hours, rising early every morning. When he retired at fifty-eight, everything changed. Ray explained that his dad just wanted to sit around the house and "do nothing." Not being active was not good for him. In just two years, his health became a problem, and he changed from "a strong man to an old man."

One afternoon, Ray was heading to the main post office in downtown Salinas. His route took him within several blocks of his mom and dad's house. Ray felt "one of those urges" to swing by their house, but he ignored the feeling. As Ray approached the post office, he recalls, "Here was a fire truck coming with lights flashing and siren screaming. I got a rather queasy feeling." So he thought he had better turn around and "see if Dad's okay." Just then, the phone rang. The message was, "Get to Dad's house...there's a big problem."

When he turned down his parents' street, he saw the fire truck in front of the house. In a panic, he rushed to the house, only to discover that his dad had died of a heart attack. Ray immediately thought, "If only I had listened to that feeling. It wouldn't have changed anything, but I could have been there for Mom."

Ray explained that from that experience with his dad, he resolved always to *listen* to God's little nudges more carefully.

Ray's story switches to the next time listening applied in his life. Ray's wife, Pam, had for years been under treatment by doctors for adult-onset asthma. She had a primary care doctor as well as an asthma specialist who was treating Pam's asthma with heavy doses of prednisone.

Pam was still getting out for shopping, hair appointments, and limited errands, but Ray could see that she was definitely slowing down. Pam was scheduled to see her doctor the following day in Ryan Ranch, which was on the road to Monterey.

Based on a urging within him, Ray announced that he was going to take her to the appointment himself. Pam was pleased. She really wasn't feeling right. Ray admits he doesn't know where this urge came from because he was very busy at work, and this was only a "regular scheduled doctor's appointment." He also pointed out that he had never taken Pam to the doctor before.

Ray was in the exam room when the nurse took Pam's vitals. She kept looking over at Ray after each reading that she took. Ray sensed that something was *not right*. When the doctor came in the exam room, he took one look at her vitals that the nurse had recorded and then asked Ray, "Who is Pam's primary care doctor?" When Ray responded that it was Dr. Heal, the doctor responded, "Here's what we are going to do: we will call Dr. Heal, and you will take Pam immediately to the emergency room at Community Hospital in Monterey. You get your wife there as soon as you can. We will have Dr. Heal meet you there."

At Community Hospital, Ray soon learned why the doctor was so concerned. Pam had a blood pressure reading of 53/27 and a heart rate of 165. Pam was in *septic shock!* The prednisone had masked an infection. It took the hospital emergency staff twenty-four hours to bring Pam back to normal.

Ray said that he still didn't realize how serious this had been, until Dr. Heal said, "It was really fortunate that you took Pam to the doctor today, because if you had arrived an hour later, she would be dead."

Ray said that he still can't explain why he chose to take Pam to the doctor that morning. "It was just something that I was supposed to do."

CHAPTER 9

The Search

———————

Story from Jaime from St. Joseph's Catholic Church in Spreckels, California

> *But we ought to give thanks to God for you always, brothers*
> *loved by the Lord, because God chose you as the first fruits for*
> *salvation through sanctification by the Spirit and belief in truth.*

2 THESSALONIANS 2:13

I HAVE HEARD IT SAID that we are all in a lifetime *search for happiness.* Some look for it in wealth, others in drugs, some in our work, some in fast cars, and some in love. It can become an endless search, with one failure after the other, because the goal of the search is misdirected.

As parents, we try to lead our children to understand that the search for happiness starts with a search for God. For this reason, we share our beliefs in God with our children. At an early age, they hear about God and learn to worship God on

Sunday and to pray before meals and before bed at night. We share God's love with the growing child, so God becomes part of his or her life.

With Jaime, God was never part of her early family life. He was never mentioned at all. Her parents were not atheists. They just were never raised with any religious belief themselves. God was not part of their lives, so God was not shared with their daughter, either. They did not do this intentionally. It was just the way it was. But God had other plans for Jaime.

When Jaime was seven years old, her best friend gave her a children's Bible full of colorful pictures and classic Bible stories. "Every night I would look through it. I stumbled across the *Our Father.* I started reading it every night before bed. No one taught me to say it every night. I just did." Perhaps, there was a certain peace that it brought her, but whatever it was, it would prove to be an important first step in her search for God.

Two years later, Jaime's parents divorced. Jaime's mother decided that what Jaime, her brother, and her sister needed now was a man in their lives to be a *father figure*, so she contacted Big Brothers and Big Sisters for help. Her mom also thought it was time to start going to church. Not knowing where to go, she asked a friend, who directed her to the Mormon Church, which they attended for about three weeks until the man working with Jaime's family as a "big brother" gave her mom a book critical of the Mormon Church's teachings. After reading just part of it, they immediately stopped going there, and at his suggestion they began attending the Vineyard Christian Fellowship Church—a charismatic Christian church.

Jaime still remembers being uncomfortable with people *speaking in tongues*, people on the floor *slain in the spirit*, and people raising their hands in praise and song, but it was her first real Christian church experience, and it would be her church until she attended the local city college.

When Jaime was thirteen, she remembers being comforted by Jesus in a vision in her bedroom in response to a long period of her sobbing. His voice was strong and clear, and his hug felt real. It took away all of her sadness and replaced it with peace. It was clear that Jaime's faith was growing. Her nightly "Our Father" continued each evening with even more fervor.

At the Vineyard, during her teenage years, Jaime attended a youth Bible study where the boys and girls studied the Bible, guided by adult leaders. She recalls that one year, when they broke into separate groups of boys and girls, the girls were asked by the pastor's wife to write down what they imagined the future qualities of their husbands would be. Here's what she wrote as a sixteen-year-old:

Jaime's Husband's Qualities:

- He would have black hair.
- He would have blue eyes
- He would wear Wranglers

❧ He would be a *country boy* (raised in the country vs. a city-type).

❧ And he must *have a heart for God.*

It was while she attended Cuesta City College that she met Paul, who attended nearby Cal Poly State University in San Luis Obispo. He was different from anyone she had ever dated. He was the first genuine *nice guy* that she had ever met. He was kind, thoughtful, and considerate. He even opened the car door for her! But he was *Catholic!* Even knowing that fact, she was still willing to date him to see what he was like. She couldn't get over the fact that he went to church every Sunday on his own. She had never known any college-age guy, when he was away from home, who attended church.

He even suggested that she join him at his church. Jaime was emphatic with her "No!" She explained to Paul that she had been taught that "Catholicism was a *cult*; the Pope was very likely *the Antichrist*, and Catholics pray to Mary." She ended this list of negatives with the following declaration, "No way will I ever set foot in *that* church." Instead of being deterred, Paul said, "Well, then let's go to *your* church." So they did.

Jaime recalls that Sunday. The preacher read the story of *David and Goliath*. After leaving the church, feeling that it had been a pretty normal service, she asked Paul what he thought. Paul's response was that the minister had stressed the bloodshed and the brutality of the killing of Goliath, rather than the true meaning of the story—putting your faith in God when you come up against great trials and in the everyday events in our life.

Jaime was taken aback. "It was like my rose-colored glasses came off." She felt that Paul was onto something, so the following Sunday, they decided to go to her best friend's parents' church. It was a Baptist or Presbyterian church...she couldn't recall. This *did not* go well, either. They both came away empty and unfulfilled. At this point, Jaime relented and said, "Fine, I'll go to your church."

Paul's church was Mission San Luis Obispo.[1] Approaching the church, Jaime was apprehensive as she remembered her words only weeks earlier—"No way will I ever set foot in *that* church!"—and here she was about to do that very thing.

Jaime described the experience in this way: "When I put my foot inside the church, I felt washed by the Holy Spirit. I knew instantly that this was where I belong." After Mass, she turned to Paul and told him, "I really like this." Paul was taken aback. He could only respond with "*Really?*"

This first Mass began a regular Sunday event for the young couple. The more Jaime attended Mass with Paul, the more she grew to love the Catholic Church. She soon joined the RCIA[2] program, which was directed by the pastor, Fr. Jim Nisbet. Paul came with her each week as her sponsor for the six months of the program. Jaime was baptized, confirmed, and received first communion at the Easter Vigil Mass in 1993.

Jaime shared that becoming Catholic completely transformed her life, and the RCIA program also helped Paul to understand elements of the Mass that he had never known before. Jaime shared, "Becoming Catholic is when my foundation started." Ten months after their first date, Paul proposed. They were married eleven months later. Interestingly enough, Paul has *black hair, blue eyes,* was *raised in the country, wears Wranglers,* and definitely has *a heart for God!*

In 2016 Jaime went to the LA Religious Education Congress as a representative of her parish. At the closing Mass, Jaime was part of the large gathering of 40,000 in attendance. Jaime found herself in the highest seat in the auditorium. As she joined the congregation in saying the "Our Father," tears began to stream down her face. She was not sobbing. These were *tears of joy!* She realized for the first time that the fulfillment of her journey in seeking God was complete in the Catholic Church.

Her journey had all started as a seven-year-old with the "Our Father," and here she was joining with forty thousand other Catholics, praying it with them as part of the closing Mass. She knew that her search was complete!

---

[1] Mission San Luis Obispo de Tolosa is a Spanish mission founded in 1772 by Father Junípero Serra in the city of San Luis Obispo, California. Today, it is a parish church in the Diocese of Monterey.

[2] RCIA (The Rite of Christian Initiation of Adults) is a process developed by the Catholic Church for prospective converts to Catholicism who are above the age of infant baptism. Candidates are introduced to aspects of Catholic beliefs and practices over a six-month process of weekly small group meetings with other interested prospective converts, as well as members of the parish. Guest speakers are often local priests or the pastor of the parish. During this period close friendships are built that provides a sense of community and welcoming, as well as a period of openness to learn about the Catholic Church.

Final acceptance into the Church normally takes place at the Easter Vigil Mass which includes the reception of Baptism (unless the person has already been baptized in another Christian faith), Confirmation, and reception of the Eucharist. For additional information – see usccb.org website.

CHAPTER 10

The Bench

———·•——

Story from Fr. Thomas P. Hall, US Navy chaplain and pastor
of Sacred Heart Army Chapel in Seaside, California

*What the Lord requires of you: only to do right and to
love goodness, and to walk humbly with your God.*

MICAH 6:8

TWENTY-FIVE YEARS AGO, FR. TOM traveled to the
Cathedral of Santiago de Compostela in northwestern
Spain, where the body of St. James the Apostle is said to be
buried. It is also the finishing point of the famous Camino de
Santiago[1] ("Way of St. James") pilgrimage. Fr. Tom and his
seminary classmate had decided to spend some time exploring
the route of this famous pilgrimage by car from the city of
Santiago de Compostela to the starting point at Saint Jean
Pied du Port, in order to get an idea what this famous pilgrim-
age was all about.

They had chosen to follow the Camino Frances, which is only one of many routes taken by pilgrims. As Fr. Tom and his classmate traveled back along the Camino, they would often stop and attend noon Mass at the old churches and basilicas in the small towns along the way. Daily, they would have a chance to sit and talk with the pilgrims, since the pilgrims were a real interest to Fr. Tom. He wanted to understand their experience. What motivated them to spend days of sometimes difficult hiking for hundreds of miles? Some of the pilgrims, he noticed, even wore medieval costumes. Fr. Tom said, "I thought that some of them were nuts!"

It is ironic that twenty-five years later, in 2010, Fr. Tom found himself one of the pilgrims hiking the Camino. After he retired from being a US Navy chaplain at sixty-two years old, Fr. Tom decided to return to France as a pilgrim himself to hike the *Camino Frances*. This time he traveled with a chaplain friend, Fr. Steve, who had also just retired.

They first flew to Paris to visit the Tours Saint-Jacque[2] on the Ile de la Cite, which is the island on the Seine River where Notre Dame Cathedral is located. Tours Saint-Jacques was originally the church that was the rallying point for the pilgrims. The church was named after St. James the Apostle, so the pilgrims would start at St. James in Paris and end at St. James in the city of Santiago de Compostela, in Spain. This spot was significant for both priests, since it gave them a sense of being part of the history of *the Camino*. They could almost imagine pilgrims gathering in the 1500s before starting off on their pilgrimage.

From Paris, the two priests traveled by train to the city of
Saint Jean Pied du Port on the border between France and
Spain. It was the traditional starting point for pilgrims to start
the *Camino Frances*.

Fr. Tom explained that the *Camino Frances* is eight hundred
kilometers long (497 miles) and is divided into three sections:

- The first section is the toughest part (133 miles) because it
  crosses over the Pyrenees Mountains.
- The second section is called the Meseta (177 miles), the
  high plains. Fr. Tom said that it is "like hiking across
  Kansas."
- The final section (187 miles) traverses the lush green hills
  and pastures of Galicia. This is the easiest section, and it
  ends in the city of Santiago de Compostela, Spain, at the
  church of St. James.

Fr. Tom and Fr. Steve each found the first part of the Camino
the most difficult. In fact, when they had traveled just forty-two miles to the third town, called Pamplona, they had to
stop. Fr. Tom had a blister on his foot "the size of Delaware."
He was concerned that it might get infected. They went to the
city hospital, where he was treated and told to stay off his feet
for one week before continuing. Fr. Steve had knee pains due to
an old high school football injury. Neither of them complained
about being forced to rest for a week. It would not only give
them a break and time to recover but a new place to explore.

When they returned to the hospital a week later, they were given the *go-ahead* to continue. They expected to pay for the doctor's exam and treatment, but they were told, "For over a thousand years, monasteries and convents have cared for the pilgrims. Today, the king of Spain pays *all* medical costs of the pilgrims." Grateful, they were soon back on the Camino, refreshed after the week of rest.

As time went by, Fr. Steve and Fr. Tom separated, each seeking the solitude of the Camino to meditate and pray as he hiked. On this particular day, Fr. Tom found himself hiking the Meseta by himself. As far as the eye could see, it was an open, flat expanse of land that stretched to the horizon. Fields of corn and clusters of cows dotted each side of the Camino. The trail was empty of pilgrims. Fr. Tom was alone.

The trail extended far into the distance, reminding him that today would be his longest day, a twenty-two-mile hike between towns. As he looked to the horizon in the west, he noticed black clouds forming. This was not a good sign because the Meseta was not where he wanted to be in a storm. There was no shelter—not even a single tree in sight—only a dirt trail and open fields. He hoped that the storm clouds would miss him. All he could do was plod onward, knowing he had a long day ahead of him that day.

As he hiked, he became lost in thought. His mind began to wander back over parts his life. He remembered the 127 US Marines he had buried at the Twenty nine Palms US Marine

Corps base during the years of the war in Iraq. He thought of his mom, whom he had buried after caring for her for the last six months of her life.

He realized that during that period of his life, he had not been able to shed even a *single tear.* He had been overwhelmed with all the losses. He now felt empty, without joy. He realized that it had been that way for a long time. Yet he continued to walk on with his head down, absorbed in his thoughts.

"The blackness started to engulf me." The sound of individual drops of rain shook him back to the problem at hand. Soon, the drops turned into a downpour. Still, he plodded along on the trail, which was now mud. He was soon soaked to the bone, but all he could do was continue to plod along.

"Okay, it's time to say the Rosary." His daily habit had been to say all twenty decades of the Rosary (the Joyful, Sorrowful, Glorious, and the Luminous mysteries) each day on his hike.

As he walked, it continued to rain. Soon his earlier thoughts returned. "I started thinking about all the guys that I had buried… and my mom. I let out a primordial scream." The rain became mixed with his tears that ran down his face. He was filled with rage and frustration. He was tired, his feet hurt, he was thirsty and hungry, but he kept going. There wasn't even a place to sit.

He made a decision that when the Rosary was finished, "I am going to sit down in the blasted mud. I am going to pull out my bottle of water and drink. I am going to take off my shoes and socks and put them in the mud. I am going to take out my peanuts and eat them. I am going to have a little feast. I don't care! I will just wallow in the mud."

When he had finally finished the twentieth decade, he began the "Hail, Holy Queen," the last prayer of the Rosary. He had plodded along, soaked, walking in the mud for so long with his eyes downcast, and now the final words of the Rosary were coming to an end:

> *To thee do we send up our sighs, mourning, and weeping in this valley of tears. Turn then, most gracious Advocate, thine eyes of mercy toward us, and after this, our exile, show unto us the blessed fruit of thy womb, Jesus. O clement, O loving, O sweet Virgin Mary! Pray for us, O holy Mother of God, that we may be made worthy of the promises of Christ.*

As he finished the prayer, he remembered he had committed to sit down when it was over...*even in the mud.* But now that the Rosary was over, he raised his eyes, and there ahead, he saw a *bench*! It was out in the middle of nowhere. What was it doing there? He sloshed over to the bench through the mud, but he no longer saw the mud. All he saw was *the bench*!

It felt wonderful to sit down, but it wasn't until he had been sitting for a while, had taken off his shoes, and was massaging his feet, that he realized he was still crying. Now his tears were tears of joy! They say that the Camino changes you. *Fr. Tom knew it was true!*

---

[1] The history of *the Camino de Santiago* goes back to the ninth century, but it did not become popular until the twelfth century. The pilgrimage to the grave of St. James was based on the tradition that St. James the Apostle had traveled to Spain to evangelize the Galicians but had returned to Jerusalem, where he was beheaded in AD 44.

His body was returned to Spain for burial. However, the boat sank in a storm off the coast of Spain, and St. James's body was found along the shore, covered with scallop shells. His body was taken to his present burial place. The scallop shells became a symbol of the Camino de Santiago pilgrimage. This is why the pilgrims, even today, wear or carry images of the scallop shell. The lines on the shell are also symbolic of the many different routes that pilgrims can follow to arrive at St. James's grave site within the great cathedral.

Today, most pilgrims want to receive a "certificate," or as it is called in Spanish, a *Compostela*, which certifies that the pilgrim did a minimum of a one-hundred-kilometer walk or two-hundred-kilometer cycling ride to the Cathedral of Santiago de Compostela.

[2] Tour Saint-Jacques is a 171-foot flamboyant Gothic tower and is all that remains of the former sixteenth-century Church of Saint-Jacques-de-la-Boucherie ("Saint James of the butchery"), which was demolished in 1797 during the French Revolution, leaving only the tower. The term *butchery* comes from the fact that the local butchers funded the cost of the church over the fourteen years of its construction.

CHAPTER 11

Philemon

———•———

Story from Tom Lukes from St. Joseph's Catholic Church in Spreckels, California, and Sacred Heart Army Chapel in Seaside, California

> *Beloved, let us love one another, because love is of God;*
> *everyone who loves is begotten by God and knows God.*
> *Whoever is without love does not know God, for God is love.*
> *In this way the love of God was revealed to us: God sent His*
> *only Son into the world so that we might have life through*
> *him. In this is love: not that we have loved God, but that he*
> *has loved us and sent his Son as expiation for our sins.*

1 JOHN 4:7–10

ST. JOSEPH'S CHURCH HAD A nine-month class during the school year for sophomore and some freshman students in preparation for confirmation in the spring. Normally, the parents of the confirmation class were asked to volunteer to teach the class, but unfortunately, at that time, no program or direction was given to these teachers as to what should be taught, and no resources were provided to help with that effort.

I was one of the four teachers who volunteered to teach the class, since my youngest son was going to be confirmed as part of the class. We had developed a list of principals that we felt were critical for our class to cover. This list would be our outline, a sort of checklist for the subject each week.

This was not the only challenge that we faced as teachers. The largest problem was to find a way to hold the attention of the forty-two young people during the one-and-one-half-hour class, a class where they really didn't want to be. We discussed many solutions to deal with this. Finally, we decided to break the students up into four small discussion groups after the lecture was over, with a list of questions for discussion, with one teacher to be part of each group. We also decided to alternate who did the teaching week after week, to offer some variety to the students, as well as to help share the teaching responsibility among the four of us.

When my turn came, I really don't remember what the topic was, but I remember deciding that I would spend half a day down at work on Saturday, catching up on work-oriented things, and half a day working on my talk at home. The previous weekend, I had developed an outline, but I was not sure about an introduction, which I had been mulling over in my mind.

I had been considering starting the teaching by telling a story, a sort of modern-day parable. The story I had created was about a man named Jack Creamer, who lived in Salinas. When he won the lottery, he decided to throw a big party for his friends. All of the people in the town wanted to come to the party, but only some were invited. Some people thought they would try and get in by going to the door and just saying that they knew Jack, but Jack only allowed people in who really knew him. The rest were turned away.

I had thought that this would be a good analogy of what would happen when we died and went to the gates of heaven. The point I was trying to make was that they needed to know Jesus and live a Christ-filled life. I just wasn't sure this was a good idea, so I decided to just let it go until later, when I would decide if I would use it or not.

So when I went to work on the Saturday of my talk preparation, I wasn't even thinking about the talk, since that was to come later at home in the afternoon. I spent about half the morning on work-related things. When I got up from my desk in the back office and headed for the front, out of my mouth came the word, "Philemon." I stopped in my tracks and repeated what I had said, "Philemon?" I thought, "What was that? Wasn't that a book in the Bible?" I could hardly wait until I got home to check it out.

Two hours later, I arrived home and immediately opened the Bible to this smallest book of the New Testament, right before Hebrews. This letter from Paul was one chapter and barely

twenty-five verses long. (I had never read the book.) I wondered what was so special about it that I had blurted out its title
out of the blue.

I sat down and read. I read the entire letter and found that the
ninth verse jumped out at me. It read, "Therefore, although I
have the full right in Christ to order you to do what is proper,
I rather urge you out of love..." (Phlm 1:9). When I read this
passage, I immediately knew that God was speaking of the
story I was thinking of telling. God did not want me to depict
Him as a cruel gatekeeper, keeping track of our sins, but rather
as a God who cared for us as His own children.

I sat down and smiled. God was again telling me something
about Himself. It was clear that He wanted me to teach these
young people that He was a loving and merciful God! It was a
good reminder to me as well. I needed to change and grow in
my view of God.

CHAPTER 12

Suzanne

Story from Suzanne Stewart from Sacred Heart Catholic Church in Salinas, California

> *Now when they heard this, they were cut to the heart, and*
> *they asked Peter and the other apostles, "What are we to do,*
> *my brothers?" Peter [said] to them: "Repent and be baptized,*
> *every one of you, in the name of Jesus Christ for the forgiveness*
> *of your sins; and you will receive the gift of the Holy Spirit."*

ACTS 2:37–38

S UZANNE WAS BORN IN ARIZONA and moved to Fresno, California, when she was four years old. She grew up with two older sisters and one younger brother. Most Sundays they attended the local Methodist church. She was raised in an anti-Catholic household, because, as Suzanne explained, "That's how my mom was raised." The family attended church on Sundays, but looking back on it. Suzanne said, "I felt that my mom and dad really didn't know Jesus at that time." This was to change in the years that followed.

Suzanne fell in love with Bob Stewart while she attended Fresno State and worked at the same finance company where Bob was employed. Bob was *Catholic!* Even with the family bias against Catholics, Bob was accepted by Suzanne's parents, perhaps because Bob no longer attended church—he was a *fallen-away Catholic.* Besides, he was a great guy!

Suzanne and Bob were married in her family's Methodist church in 1963. They began their first year of marriage in Monterey, California, where Bob's job had required him to move. In the early years of marriage, they never attended church.

During this time, Suzanne's mom had a conversion experience that changed her into a *fired-up Christian,* much to her daughter's surprise. Her mom began attending a Pentecostal church in Fresno. As a result of her newly found zeal, for birthdays and Christmas her mom started sending Suzanne and Bob Christian books.

Bob and Suzanne were so far from God at this time that Suzanne recalls that they even made fun of her mom's sudden conversion. They never read any of the fifteen or more books that she had sent them over the years. They simply found a bottom drawer to hide them in.

It was about this time that Suzanne joined a women's book club in Salinas. The club's goal was to read one book a month and then get together to discuss that book at the monthly meeting. Through this process Suzanne read a variety of popular novels selected by the members of the club. One day, someone suggested that they read a bestselling Christian book by Hal Lindsey called *The Late Great Planet Earth.*

This book examined Bible prophesies of the *end times* and its coming fulfillment. It suggested that the end of the world would come in the 1970s. The book made the readers fearful of the coming end of the world and challenged them to read the Bible to see these prophesies. It was this book that Suzanne said really affected her.

When Suzanne's friend Shirley Swanson heard that the book club was going to discuss *The Late Great Planet Earth*, she wanted to come because, although she had not read the book, she had heard about it, and she wanted to hear the discussion about this well-known book. Well into the discussion, Shirley shared her simple approach to Christianity with Suzanne and the group. "All you have to do is invite Jesus into your heart, and He will come."

Suzanne had never heard this before. "I was just stunned!" She repeated in her mind Shirley's simple statement: "All you have to do is invite Jesus into your heart, and He will come." In that moment of faith, something immediately happened to her. She announced to the group that she had to leave. She got up with her baby, Michael, and went to her car, where she put Michael in his infant carrier.

As she sat in her car, she began crying and sobbing for her sins. She didn't understand what was happening. "I had never considered myself a sinner, because I was a nice person, and I knew people that were worse than me." She realized that in sinning, she had offended God. Her tears continued for what seemed like a long time. Soon the crying and sobbing turned to joyful laughter when she realized what had just happened to her. She didn't know what was going on, but she felt compelled to get home.

Since Bob was away on a trip to Utah and would be gone for three days, she decided to read those Christian books her mom had sent her. So for next three days, between feeding and taking care of her three young boys, Suzanne read and read and read some more. "I couldn't put them down." She didn't sleep for three days. She immersed herself in these books. When Bob came back, she returned the books to the drawer, since she was afraid to tell him what had happened to her: *She had become a Christian!*

The next morning when Bob left for work, Suzanne called a Christian friend, who came over. Suzanne needed help. All the books she had read included quotes from the Bible, so she wanted her friend to help her with the Bible. Where to start? What does it mean? So they ended up reading the Bible together. For days they read the Bible while Bob was at work.

When Bob came home after work, "We would put the Bible away and just act normally." After that week of Bible reading with her friend, Suzanne continued reading by herself whenever she could find time. Soon she had read the entire Bible.

Studying the Bible became a regular thing for her. Soon she even began to memorize key verses that had special meaning to her, like John 3:16: "God so loved the world that He gave us His only Son, that whoever believes in Him should not perish, but have eternal life."

Within a few years, Suzanne and Bob attended a *Cursillo*[1] at St. Francis Camp in Seascape. Since a Cursillo was a religious weekend experience, it was difficult to talk Bob into attending it. Suzanne's friends had attended a Cursillo and loved it, so she was determined to go. Fortunately, Bob loved Suzanne, and although he didn't want to go, he knew he had to go, especially since, according to the Cursillo rules, both had to go. Bob backed out on the first two scheduled weekends, but eventually, he went.

"It was a miracle that he got there at all," Suzanne said.

Suzanne attended the men's closing Mass on Sunday afternoon, which was the conclusion of the men's Cursillo. The Mass was especially joyful and spirited. When it was concluded, greetings and hugs were shared as Bob joined the family to head home.

Their son, Timothy, noticed his dad's twelve-inch-long hand-made nametag hung around his neck in the shape of a fish. Since Bob was an avid fisherman and often went fishing with his boys, little Timothy wanted to know, "Did you go fishing, Dad?"

Bob said, "Yeah, sort of."

Timothy responded, "Did you catch anything?"

Bob replied, "No, I got caught."

Bob did get caught up in the net of Jesus's love as shared on that Cursillo. It was one thing to be told, "God loves you," but it is quite another thing to experience it firsthand. Suzanne was happy to have Bob share in her joy of Christianity. He was a new person—the Cursillo Weekend had been *life changing*.

After Cursillo, Suzanne and Bob began attending the Saturday vigil Mass at Sacred Heart Church in Salinas with the family. However, Suzanne was having serious doubts about the Catholic faith. For this reason, she also attended the local Lutheran church in the morning, while the kids attended Sunday school there.

Her early anti-Catholic upbringing contributed to her doubts about some teachings of the Catholic faith. This even showed up in her sometimes-heated debates with her Catholic lady friends on issues especially related to Mary. She questioned the teachings on the Immaculate Conception, the perpetual virginity of Mary, and the idea that Mary was the mother of all Christians.

She really was searching for answers, when Fr. Jim Nisbet offered a class for those seeking information about the Catholic faith. (This was before the RCIA program was established.) Both Catholics and non-Catholics were invited to attend the meetings that were to be held at her parish, so Suzanne decided to attend.

Fr. Jim Nisbet was well-known for his knowledge of scripture and his teaching gifts. But during these classes, Suzanne was afraid to ask Fr. Jim questions; instead, she decided to just be open to his teaching and hope that he would address her concerns and that she would learn more about the Catholic faith.

Her doubts on the dogma of the Immaculate Conception were cleared up when Fr. Jim explained that the words in Greek (*kekaritomene*) for "full of grace" should be translated as "never without grace." These are the words that the angel called Mary: "Hail full of grace, the Lord is with you" (Lk 1:28). This was his proof that Mary was never *with sin*, because she was always *full of grace*. Fr. Jim explained that *sin* was the *absence of grace*, or to put it another way, if you were always *full of grace*, you could not have sinned.

Suzanne had always questioned Mary's perpetual virginity because the Bible said that Jesus had brothers and sisters, but Fr.

Jim explained that there wasn't a word for *cousins* in Aramaic, so they used the word for *brothers* and *sisters*. He further pointed out that when Jesus was on the cross, Jesus gave Mary to be cared for by the apostle John. This would not have been necessary if Mary had other children—one of her children would have taken care of Mary. In fact, it would have been an insult to Jesus's family members to ask John to care for her. "And from that hour the disciple took her to his own home" (Jn 19:27).

She also learned that when Jesus said, "Woman, behold your son!" Then he said to the disciple, "Behold, your mother (Jn 19:27)!" This made Mary the mother of us all. Fr. Jim explained that just as Jesus put Mary in the care of John—and John in the care of Mary—so too, we, like John, are placed in Mary's care as her children.

God's timing was perfect. Just as Suzanne was looking for answers, Fr. Jim began his class. His teaching opened her eyes to new truths of Catholicism and showed her the beauty and depth of the faith. She was received into the Church in 1979 and remains a fired-up Catholic ever since.

---

[1] Cursillo is a Roman Catholic movement that was founded in Majorca, Spain, in 1944 as a three-day weekend retreat for men to prepare them to participate in the *Camino de Santiago pilgrimage*. It was also intended to bring the men back to church.

Cursillo has been declared by the Catholic Church as a *charism of the Holy Spirit*. It was so successful that the women insisted on being included. Later, the Catholics invited their Christian brothers and sisters to join them. Eventually, Catholics and other Christian faiths split into separate weekends— one Catholic and one Anglican.

Cursillo consists of a series of short talks given by the lay team members and one or more priests who act as spiritual directors. The men attend on one weekend, with the women attending the following weekend. The candidates and team arrive on Thursday after work, but the Cursillo formally begins on Friday. The three-day experience ends Sunday afternoon.

CHAPTER 13

Monica's Letter

Story from Suzanne Stewart from Sacred Heart Catholic Church in Salinas, California

We know that all things work for the good of those who love God, who are called according to His purpose.

ROMANS 8:28

NEARLY TWENTY YEARS AFTER HER Cursillo experience and becoming Catholic, Suzanne faced a crisis in her life. She had cancer!

All her friends came forward with their support by bringing meals, running errands, shopping, and even taking the kids to sports' practices. "They really helped me cope. I am not sure we could have made it without their help." Her friends assured Suzanne that she was going to be healed. She knew that healing was possible but asked, "Why would I be singled out for healing?" This led her to be so focused on being healed that it only added more stress to an already stressed life.

With healing at the forefront of Suzanne's thinking, she decided to attend a *Healing Mass* at St. Joseph's Church in Spreckels. Fr. Bain from the diocese of San Francisco was the gifted celebrant. At the conclusion of Mass, Fr. Bain prayed over everyone who came forward. However, it was his words during his homily that really affected Suzanne. This is what she wrote in her journal: "Fr. Bain said, 'Our purpose in life is not to be *healed*. It is *to become like Jesus*. Whether you are sick or well, we can do the will of the Father.'"

These words changed Suzanne's focus from her healing to becoming more like Jesus. Fr. Bain had said becoming more like Jesus is the *purpose* in our life. Suzanne thought, "Whether I live or die, I wasn't going to let it interfere with me drawing closer to Jesus." This helped Suzanne face her first bout with cancer. She went through the normal chemotherapy treatment for weeks, and finally the cancer was gone.

It took some time to feel right again. Her hair did grow back, and normalcy returned to her life and her family's life. Most importantly, Suzanne came away from this experience with a renewed closeness to Jesus, whom she had so depended on during this entire struggle.

Checkups continued on a regular basis after she was free of cancer. After eighteen months of good health, Suzanne returned to the doctor for her normal checkup and CT scan. The staff was friendly, cheerful, and happy to see her well and returning to normal life. She had moved on with her life. She never feared that the cancer might return, which Suzanne credited as a grace from God. This led to great joy that was always evident in her countenance.

Several days after her doctor's visit, Suzanne called the office for the results of her CT scan. The nurse put her on hold while she spoke to the doctor. When she returned the nurse told Suzanne, "The doctor would like to see you." *This was not what Suzanne wanted to hear.* "I knew what it meant. If everything was fine, they would have told me over the phone." Obviously, everything was not fine. "And so, after how close I had come to Jesus, this terrible fear came over me."

She returned to work. It was noon. Still overcome with fear, she decided to go home for lunch. The first thing she did was check the mail, even though the mailman usually didn't come until 4:00 p.m. To her surprise, not only was there mail, but the mail included a thick envelope from a dear young friend, Monica.

Suzanne had met Monica at a summer camp where Suzanne had been a counselor for teenagers. Monica had been a high school student in Phoenix. At the camp they had immediately become close. "We just connected. We became the best of friends." Through letters, their relationship continued in the years that followed. Monica was now twenty-two years old.

Suzanne was soon engrossed in reading Monica's five-page letter, with all thoughts of the nurse's message gone from her mind. Monica's words were exactly what Suzanne needed to hear. Monica wrote of "a wonderful renewal she had with Jesus, including details of the vision she had of Jesus coming toward her, holding out his arms saying, 'Come, come. I will lead you to eternal life.'" Monica went on to write, "Mrs. Stewart, God has made it clear to me that *my life is not my own. It is His.* He is the one who gave me life, and he can take it away when He pleases. So I must live my life to honor Him. Life is difficult but bearable with Jesus as my hope."

Monica concluded her letter with the question, "Oh by the way, Mrs. Stewart, how are you doing?" The answer was that Suzanne was doing much, much better because of the joy that Monica expressed in her letter and the message that stuck with Suzanne: "I must live to honor Him." Suzanne could picture Monica's vision of Christ and His message: "Come, come. I will lead you to eternal life."

That afternoon, Suzanne went into the doctor's office. She immediately noticed that the staff was more reserved in their attitude toward her. "They were all looking at me. Everyone gave me that sad look." Suzanne, on the other hand, was still on a cloud of joy. Nothing could upset her. Suzanne was taken to an exam room to wait for her doctor.

Dr. Flanagan came into the room. "I am afraid I have a little bit of bad news. The cancer is back..." he said. "Don't worry about it. Everything will be fine!" Suzanne heard herself say, but she wasn't sure who was talking. What had happened to all that fear? Monica's letter had changed everything.

Suzanne left the doctor's office that day still joyful. She knew the coming weeks would be tough, but now she reflected back on Monica's letter. "My life is not my own. It is His. He is the one who gave me life, and he can take it away when He pleases, so I must live my life to honor Him. Life is difficult but bearable with Jesus as my hope."

The treatment of Suzanne's cancer meant weeks of chemotherapy that not only caused loss of her hair but resulted in a low blood count. This meant that she was especially susceptible to infection or any contagious disease. She basically had lost her ability to fight off any sickness. She needed to take special precautions for what she touched and to avoid contact with people.

The doctor's report of low blood count came on the Monday before her son Timothy's wedding.

The doctor told her that she could attend the wedding, but she would have to wear a mask. The image of her attending her son's wedding wearing a mask didn't sit well with Suzanne. She didn't want to appear that she was seeking sympathy. "Oh, look at poor Suzanne. She is suffering so!" Initially, she decided she just wouldn't attend, if that was what she had to do. She would stay home.

Suzanne's friend Mary Beth decided to ask Fr. Patrick Dooling to celebrate a *Healing Mass* for Suzanne and the other sick parishioners in the area. So, on the Wednesday before the wedding, Suzanne went to the Healing Mass. She sat alone next to an open window so that the only air she breathed was the fresh outside air, as her doctor had advised. She was extremely careful to avoid contact with anyone, except for *the laying on of hands* by Fr. Patrick. Everything seemed to go well.

On Friday, she returned to the doctor for another blood test. The doctor said that for some reason her white blood count had returned to normal. He could not explain the change, but *Suzanne knew!*

The positive results of the blood test allowed Suzanne to be a part of her son's wedding and reception without the mask, but it did not mean she was healed of cancer. So on the day following the wedding, Suzanne traveled to UCLA Medical Center for a bone marrow transplant. The more-than-a-month-long treatment was the most difficult Suzanne had experienced so far. At one point, she was not sure that she would ever make it home. But she did make it.

The first CT scan following her return showed that she was free of cancer. A great "Alleluia!" went up from her friends and family! She was so happy to have that experience behind her and return to her family—cancer free.

NOTE: in 2017 Suzanne and her husband, Bob, still live in

Salinas. This year they celebrated their fifty-fourth year of marriage. The cancer did return on two occasions, but she has been cancer-free for the past ten years and is in good health. And *Joy* is still very much a part of her life!

CHAPTER 14

Storms in Life

———•—•———

Story from Tom Lukes from St. Joseph's Catholic Church in Spreckels, California, and Sacred Heart Army Chapel in Seaside, California.

"Footprints"

One night I dreamed a dream.
As I was walking along the beach with my Lord.
Across the dark sky flashed scenes from my life.
For each scene, I noticed two sets of footprints in the sand,
One belonging to me and one to my Lord.
After the last scene of my life flashed before me,
I looked back at the footprints in the sand.
I noticed that at many times along the path of my life,
especially at the very lowest and saddest times,
there was only one set of footprints.
This really troubled me, so I asked the Lord about it.
"Lord, you said once I decided to follow you,
You'd walk with me all the way.

But I noticed that during the saddest
and most troublesome times of my life,
there was only one set of footprints.
I don't understand why,
when I needed You the most, You would leave me."
He whispered, "My precious child,
I love you and will never leave you
never, ever, during your trials and testings.
When you saw only one set of footprints,
It was then that I carried you.

MARY STEVENSON

IT WAS LATE, THE SAN Francisco Giants had just won, the interview was over, and so I turned off the TV. For some reason, my hand went to my chest. I was just feeling what was there. Why I did this I do not know. I didn't feel any tenderness...nothing initiated this action, but what I did feel was *a lump*. I decided I needed to show this to my general practitioner, Dr. Douglas Cambier—*and soon*.

Fortunately, I have known Doug for more than thirty years. He attended the same church, and our boys had played baseball together. But how was I going to talk to him about possible breast cancer? Should I tell my wife, Lois, or just make the appointment and make some excuse to her for being late coming back after weekday Mass? I didn't want to worry her without reason. If it were cancer, what would that mean? I knew that would not be a good thing—surgery, followed by chemotherapy probably.

My mom and sister both had had breast cancer. The thought went through my mind, "Why didn't I tell Doug about my family history on earlier visits?" My Mom was ninety-one when they performed a lumpectomy on her breast. The results came back that it was an aggressive cancer, and they wanted to do a mastectomy. Mom refused. She said that she was ready to die, so she didn't want to go through the pain and suffering for what, a few more years? (Two years later, Mom did die, but not from cancer.)

I was sure that I would have to go through the male version of a mastectomy, go through chemotherapy, and probably lose my hair. With these thoughts racing through my mind, I experienced a rather troubled sleep, but I couldn't talk to my wife about this. No sense in both of us losing sleep over it!

I decided to call Dr. Doug on the way to church Monday morning and make an appointment. I would not tell Lois for now. I was able to get an appointment at the doctor's office on Wednesday. Wouldn't you know it—the person who took the appointment was a close friend from church. I really didn't want to explain my breast lump to her right then, so I was vague about why the appointment was necessary.

Wednesday morning, after church, I was heading to Doug's office. I decided to call home and let Lois know why I would be late getting home. She understood, and she did not sound frightened or apprehensive, although I was.

I sat in the waiting room, thinking about what was important to tell Doug: family histories, concern for privacy, ask about treatment. (I should point out that I was convinced I had breast cancer. It was just another thing that came with getting older.)

After taking my weight, I was led into the exam room. The nurse asked me why I was there. I replied that it was *a private matter* that I wished to discuss with Dr. Cambier. When Dr. Doug arrived, he found me sitting at the edge of the exam table with my shirt already off. *I wanted to get this behind me.* I explained the family history and how I had discovered the lump in my chest. Doug said that this sometimes happens, even in men. He asked me to lie down on the raised exam table. I directed Doug to the lump. He said that he could feel what I was talking about. I sat up.

The next words from Doug would be critical. I expected that I would have to have a biopsy, but instead Doug said that he wanted me to have a *mammogram*! He filled in a referral form and told me that it might be a couple of weeks before I could get in to the Nancy Ausonio Mammography Center. I was shocked! *This was bad!* I don't know why I had not anticipated this. I couldn't imagine sitting in the waiting room with a bunch of women, who would wonder why I was there.

Doug said that they would probably have to do *a biopsy*. Doug showed me the size of the needle that would be used to take the biopsy. He used the inside ink tube of a ballpoint pen to indicate the size of the needle. He said that they would use a *sonogram* to carefully locate the tumor to help guide the needle. It didn't look too bad. I was more concerned about facing the women at the Mammography Center, and all those women in the waiting room. Ugh!

On the way home, I called Lois to tell her the news. I guess I really gave her a scare, when I slipped up and told her I was going to have to have a *mastectomy* instead of a *mammogram*. I immediately corrected myself after Lois said, "What?" But it was too late; I had shocked her!

When she had caught her breath, Lois suggested that I should *not go* to the center that Doug had suggested, because it is always really busy and full of women in the waiting room. It was more of a *spa atmosphere*. I should instead go to the Monterey Mammography Center, which was a much smaller facility.

Later that day, we drove together to Monterey so that I could make the appointment and make sure that the physician order, which Doug had written for the Ausonio Center in Salinas, would still be acceptable at the Monterey Mammography Center. My other goal was to collect any forms that would need to be filled out so that I could fill them out at home, rather than to do so in the waiting room. I was still fearful of sitting in a mammography center waiting room.

Fortunately, when I entered the Monterey Mammography Center, the small waiting room was empty, and the woman at the desk was very sweet and understanding. I expressed my embarrassment at being there, and she assured me that this is not that unusual. "More than likely you will be just fine." I liked her attitude.

My appointment was in six days. The waiting would be the tough part. I started to feel better about it, especially since the waiting room was so small. I just accepted that surgery would probably be necessary, but I could handle that. I would move on and hope that the cancer had not spread.

The following Tuesday morning, the day of my appointment finally came. We had already said three Rosaries. I headed to Mass at St. Joseph's Church in Spreckels. I arrived twenty minutes early to allow for some time for prayer and reading from the "Magnificat." I sat alone, and I prayed for help from God.

I opened the "Magnificat" to the readings for Mass for that day, June 30, 2015. When I had read them, I turned to the "Meditation of the Day." This was what I read on the day of my mammogram:

"How to Face the Storms in Life"

> *Do not look forward in fear to the changes in life; rather,*
> *look to them with full hope that as they arise, God, whose*
> *very own you are, will lead you safely through all things; and*
> *when you cannot stand it, God will carry you in his arms.*

*Do not fear what may happen tomorrow; the same
understanding Father who cares for you today will take care
of you then and every day. He will shield you from suffering
or will give you unfailing strength to bear it. Be at peace
and put aside all anxious thought and imaginations.*

SAINT FRANCIS DE SALES

I could not have asked for anything more from God that morning. I could now go forward and face whatever was in store for me, because the message was comforting. *Praise God!!*

NOTE: no lump was found on the mammogram, much to my relief!

CHAPTER 15

God Provides

Story from Margaret and Ray Tellez from Sacred Heart
Catholic Church in Salinas, California

> *Ask and it will be given to you; seek and you will find; knock and*
> *the door will be opened to you. For everyone who asks, receives;*
> *and the one who seeks, finds; and to the one who knocks, the door*
> *will be opened. Which one of you would hand his son a stone when*
> *he asks for a loaf of bread, or a snake when he asks for a fish?*

MATTHEW 7:7–11

MARGARET AND RAY HAD BEEN married for sixty-four years
when they shared their story with me. Margaret was
eighty-four and Ray eighty-seven, but to really appreciate their
story you need to first learn something about each of them.

Margaret was the fifth of seven children. Family pictures of
her relatives in their home date back to the 1800s. At the age
of fourteen, Margaret had to drop out of school to work in the

cannery to help feed the family during the Depression. This may explain why she grew up with a desire to reach out and help those in need and also to trust that God would provide for their needs. Margaret said that she has always loved everybody. "I was born that way."

Ray grew up in the Los Angeles area and served in World War II. He was a cook in the US Army. When the war was over, he went to work as a chef in Los Angeles. This meant leaving at 5:00 a.m. to get to work on time. As a loving wife, Margaret always got up with him to get his breakfast and be with him when he started his day. Ray worked until he was seventy-nine, which included forty years as chef for the Dal Rae Restaurant in Pico Rivera, a suburb of Los Angeles.

Margaret shared with me the story of how God worked in their lives during their sixty-four years of marriage. God always seemed to provide for their food needs, sometimes in the most surprising ways.

One warm summer day, when Margaret was out in the backyard, she noticed that her neighbor's plum tree was full of ripe plums. She couldn't help but think about how good a cold, sweet plum would taste. Even though the thought persisted, she put it out of her mind and went in the house. Hours later, Ray arrived home from work with a bag of plums even larger than her neighbor's. Ray explained to his wife that someone had just dropped by the restaurant with them. He wanted Ray to have them.

Another time, Margaret was helping a ninety-two-year-old friend with her shopping, as she did every week. This lady friend wanted to maintain her independence by doing her own shopping, but she could no longer drive, so Margaret would drive her to the market where they would each take a cart and head off in different directions to shop. This particular day, Margaret was planning to purchase some beef shank for soup, but she found the selection limited, so she decided to wait until another day.

She found herself in line at the checkout counter behind her elderly friend, who she noticed had bought some great looking corn on the cob. She could not go back after corn, because there were other people behind her in line, and her friend would be forced to wait for her, so Margaret decided to wait until another day. As if God was working directly with Ray, again Ray arrived home with a bag of only two items: three pounds of beef shank steak and some corn on the cob.

Another time, Margaret asked Ray to stop on the way home from work to pick up some Jell-O for her. When he arrived home, he announced that a salesman had stopped by work and asked Ray to try a new flavor of Jell-O he was now selling, so he didn't even have to go to the store.

And still another time, Margaret asked Ray to pick up some watermelon at the store, but again one of his restaurant staff came to work with two watermelons that he gave to Ray to take home.

Finally, Margaret related a similar story. This time when Ray arrived home she realized that she had forgotten to ask Ray to stop at the store and buy some tortillas. She apologized for not thinking of it before he left work. She then asked Ray if he would run to the store for tortillas. Ray said, "Oh, thanks for reminding me. I forgot I have three dozen tortillas in the car that someone gave me."

In 1996, Ray retired from the restaurant business at the age of seventy-nine. Ray and Margaret began to think of finding a home closer to their daughter in Carmel Valley. They had seen a condo complex called Cambridge Village in Salinas that they liked, but no two-bedroom homes were available at that time, so they went back to Los Angeles.

Margaret urged Ray to put up their house for sale. Ray asked the logical question, "What will we do if we sell our house before we find a place in Salinas?" This made a lot of sense to Ray, because they were living in Los Angeles and were not able to look for a house in Salinas from such a distance. Margaret responded, "Don't worry. The Lord will provide for us."

About two years passed with their house on and off the market, but their house did not sell. One day, Margaret's daughter in Carmel Valley called with news that a two-bedroom condo in Cambridge Village was advertised for sale. She asked her mom and dad if they wanted her to go take a look at it for them. Margaret said not only that she should, but also if she liked it, to put $1,000 down to hold it. Later that evening, Margaret and Ray heard from their daughter that she had liked the house and had put the money down. Ray said, "Now what are we going to do?" Margaret's response was, "Don't worry. That means we are going to sell our house!" Sure enough, their house sold the next week!

It is clear that Margaret's experiences throughout her life have helped her to trust in God. As far as Margaret is concerned, if you really believed in God, you should naturally expect God to act on your behalf, whether it is a matter of something as small as a plum, or as important as selling your house when you need to. Faith and trust in God had become Margaret's way of life.

CHAPTER 16

The Icon

Story from Cheryl Ward-Kaiser from St. Joseph's Catholic
Church in Spreckels, California

> *When the wine ran short, the mother of Jesus said to him,*
> *"They have no wine." [And] Jesus said to her, "Woman, how*
> *does your concern affect me? My hour has not yet come. " His*
> *mother said to the servers, "Do whatever he tells you."*

JOHN 2:3–5

CHERYL HAD COME TO THE New Camaldoli Hermitage
for the sole purpose of dealing with a question that
had troubled her for many months. Should she continue
on staff at the Crisis Pregnancy Center (CPC) or return
to volunteer work with the youth ministry in her parish?
She had hoped to find *a quiet place* in the church to pray
for guidance in this decision that was weighing so heavily
on her soul. "I walked around the corner, and there she
was."—A single light illuminated *a beautiful icon* of Our

Lady of Perpetual Help[1] on the wall. A single chair and kneeler was near-by.

The image was very striking: Mary is holding baby Jesus, while angels can be seen in the upper left and upper right of Mary. These figures are all set on a background of gold, which adds to the visual impact of the icon.

As she sat there in silence, she realized that the image of Mary holding baby Jesus reminded her of her two choices:

- Working with the youth at Madonna del Sasso Church youth camp. (The great experience of seeing the transformation of young people called *Covenant Camp*.) or
- Helping to save babies at CPC

Covenant Camp was the result of a full year of planning and sacrifice. She remembered the challenge of dealing with eighty, seventh and eighth graders, both Catholic and non-Catholic boys and girls. The camp lasted an entire week, culminating in a *reconciliation service* where a handful of priests heard the confessions of these young people. The camp provided a week of fun for the kids, and it provided life-changing spiritual growth for them as well.

Her work with the youth was especially meaningful to Cheryl. She really wanted to go back to work with the youth, but she also knew that her work at the Crisis Pregnancy Center was very important. She was torn between the two.

Cheryl recalled the first phone call from Bishop Shubsda a few years earlier. He shared his concern for the present Seaside CPC staff—all non-Catholics. They were using the women's pregnancy crisis to talk some of the women seeking counseling away from the Catholic Church. The bishop said that this needed to change in the new CPC.

Bishop Shubsda wanted to start a CPC in Salinas that would have an all-Catholic staff of volunteers to both serve the women in crisis and to represent the Catholic Church in this ministry. Cheryl's *yes* to the bishop meant walking away from her more-than-ten-year involvement in youth ministry at Madonna del Sasso Church, yet the bishop had made it clear how important this was to him and to the diocese, so she had agreed.

Training soon followed to prepare Cheryl and other volunteers to allow them to counsel the women in facing a pregnancy crisis. The training was thorough and helpful, but Cheryl still felt inadequate. "I can't do this. I will just go in and answer the phone."

The opening day found Cheryl and two other volunteers staffing the CPC. They anxiously awaited their first visitors. Cheryl's plan of just answering the phone immediately fell apart when three women came at once. The first two women went into the counseling rooms, leaving the last woman waiting with Cheryl.

Cheryl knew instinctively that she could not wait for another counselor to be available. She was afraid the woman might flee. In fact, she was not a woman but a *young girl*. Cheryl soon learned she was fourteen years old! Her story of how she became pregnant through incest was beyond Cheryl's comprehension—it angered Cheryl. Cheryl felt inadequate to deal with her. She didn't know even what to say. How could this have happened?

She knew that by law that she would have to report it to the police, but right now Cheryl needed to help this girl with her crisis. What could she say? "I was sweating bullets, and I was praying so hard. 'God, you are going to have to give me help with this. What in the world am I doing in this room with this girl?'" She realized that all she could do was to show her love. Now, she knew what to say. She spoke to her of love—the love that God had for her and the love as a mother she should have for her child.

Cheryl had taken on the role of a loving mother as if this young girl were her own daughter sharing with her mom her fears and hurt. Cheryl simply showed her love and compassion. Finally, when she left, Cheryl didn't know what the outcome would be, but she knew that she had done all she could to help her. It was now in God's hands.

Cheryl's follow-up phone call revealed that the young girl had suffered a miscarriage. Cheryl's first thought was that perhaps this might be best under the circumstances, although it still was not what Cheryl had even thought about during her counseling.

This first experience at the CPC was nothing that she could have anticipated. Looking back on it now, it had turned out to be the most difficult counseling that she had done in all the years that followed. It was like a baptism of fire!

Over the years at CPC, she had seen successes and failures. What was so frustrating for her was that "The ones I thought that I had made a difference and I thought they would carry, they aborted; and the ones I thought that I had done a terrible job...it would never work, they would carry." This was not just another job; it meant everything to Cheryl. "I grieved the loss of those children. It was unbelievable! We would comfort each other, but it still was difficult to deal with it day after day."

Mary continued to look down from the icon on the wall in front of Cheryl. It was as if Mary was just waiting. Finally, Cheryl returned from her memories and prayed for an answer. "What I really was asking was to let me out of this. I don't want to do it anymore. It's too heavy! It is too much!!" Then, "I heard an audible voice saying, '*Cheryl*, will you take care of my babies?' I got so caught up with the fact that she [Mary] said my name that I almost forgot whatever else she said."

"I left knowing full well what I had to do. I needed to stay with it." Encouraged by Mary's words, Cheryl returned to CPC and continued to work there for over ten years. She will always remember that Mary addressed her by name as she sat in front of the icon of Our Lady of Perpetual Help.

---

[1] "Our Lady of Perpetual Help" is a title of the Blessed Virgin Mary, as represented in a celebrated fifteenth-century Byzantine icon. The icon has been in Rome since 1499 and is permanently enshrined in the church of Saint Alfonso di Liguori.

In the Eastern Orthodox Church, this artistic iconography is known as "Theotokos" ("Mother of God") or the "Virgin of the Passion," due to the instruments of the Passion present on the image. The angels are Michael and Gabriel (Source: Wikipedia).

CHAPTER 17

Lourdes: Holy Ground

———◆———

Story from Pete Felice from San Carlos Borromeo Cathedral
in Monterey, California

> *When the Lord saw him coming over to look at it more closely, God*
> *called out to him from the bush, "Moses! Moses!" He answered,*
> *"Here I am." God said, "Come no nearer! Remove the sandals*
> *from your feet, for the place where you stand is holy ground."*

ExODUS 3:4–5

IT HAD ALL STARTED AS a result of an annual mammogram
for Barbara. A small lump was discovered. The biopsy that
followed revealed that it was an aggressive form of cancer. A
lumpectomy to remove the cancer as well the affected lymph
nodes was performed at Community Hospital of Monterey
(CHOMP). Three weeks later, Barbara began chemotherapy. It was the harshest chemotherapy treatment available for
breast cancer at that time.

The chemotherapy consisted of an eighteen-day cycle followed by an eighteen-day break to allow Barbara to recover from the effects of the chemo. This cycle of eighteen days of therapy and eighteen days recovery was to be repeated over the next seven-month period.

By the end of the first eighteen-day treatment, Barbara was really feeling exhausted and sick. It was hard for Barbara to imagine that this was to continue for *seven months*! But after the eighteen-day recovery period, she was feeling better. She was ready to start again. It had been a very difficult time for Barbara, and even Pete was affected with the stress of seeing his wife suffer so.

Months later, as the last days of chemotherapy treatment were coming to an end, a friend suggested to Barbara that she should consider a trip to celebrate the completion of her treatments. When Barbara mentioned it to Pete, he responded without hesitation, "Tell me where you want to go, and I will take you there." But Barbara had no idea where she wanted to go. She just wanted to get away—but where?

The one consolation during the chemotherapy treatments was that St. Angela's Catholic Church in Pacific Grove was only a fifteen-minute drive from CHOMP. So every day after her morning treatments, Barbara was able to attend daily Mass.

The day after she spoke to Pete about the trip, she noticed a bulletin board announcement at the back of church that she had never seen before. It described a pilgrimage to the holy sites of Paris, with the final four days to be spent in Lourdes. This sounded *wonderful*! Could this be the answer?

Her immediate concern was that, according to the flyer, the trip was only three weeks away. The pastor, Fr. Jerry McCormick, told her to check with the Pacific Grove Travel Agency to see if there were any seats remaining. Even if there were still seats available, three weeks would be a short amount of time to get their passports.

At the travel agency, Barbara learned that there were still seats available. They were the last two seats. It was meant to be! She only hoped it was not too late to get their passports in time. Barbara knew that if God wanted her to go, He would make it happen. So far, everything was going their way.

As it turned out, Barbara and Pete were able to get passports and shop for everything that they would need on the trip in the three weeks remaining. She had always wanted to go to Lourdes! Fr. Jerry would be leading the pilgrimage, and he was one of her favorite priests. *God is great*!

To make it even better, Pete and Barbara also discovered that two of their close friends, Jerry and Gerry Carnazzo, were also part of the group. They had known the Carnazzos from Cursillo, and they looked forward to sharing the pilgrimage experience with them. This was an added blessing.

Paris was not just a city of lights, museums, and great food, but the Paris part of the pilgrimage included daily Mass and a chance to visit the holy sites, most of which Barbara and Pete were not even aware of. They visited the Shrine of St. Vincent de Paul and the Royal Chapel at Versailles. Fr. Jerry even celebrated Mass at Notre Dame Cathedral, which they learned was built before America was even discovered, and it took four hundred years to build!

The highlight of their stay in Paris was within sight of the Eiffel Tower, on a small side street called Rue de Bac, at the Chapel of Our Lady of the Miraculous Medal. This chapel was where Our Lady appeared to St. Catherine Labouré in a series of apparitions in 1830. At one of the apparitions, Mary asked Catherine to have a medal cast of Mary's image. The medal became known as The Miraculous Medal[1] because of the many miracles that happened once it was released.

Leaving Paris behind, the pilgrimage group traveled by bullet train across the farmland for the five-and-one-half-hour trip to Lourdes, which is nestled in the foothills of the Pyrenees. Lourdes has a population of about fifteen thousand and is located in southern France. More than five million pilgrims come there each year to visit the place where Mary appeared to Bernadette Soubirous in 1858 when she was just fourteen years old.

Lourdes is especially known for its miraculous healing waters, which are what drew Barbara and Pete to Lourdes initially. It is said that there are two types of miracles that take place at Lourdes: *healings* and *cures*. *Healings* are said to be emotional cures—that is, help to accept a serious illness or problem—whereas *cures* are physical healing—that is, the disease is gone. Pete wanted Barbara's cancer to be gone, while Barbara was open to whatever God had planned for her. "Not my will, but yours be done" (Lk 22:42).

The grounds of the grotto are referred to as *the Sanctuary of Our Lady of Lourdes* or simply *the domain*. It consists of 125 acres that include many churches and chapels. The Gave de Pau River divides the site. Multiple bridges are used by pilgrims to access the Church of St. Bernadette and other parts of the domain on the other side of this large river. In the distance, a large Roman fort can be seen on the highest hill of the city, with a flag waving on the single tower that remains.

From the city of Lourdes, you enter the domain through one of two gates: *the St. Joseph's Gate* or *the St. Michael Gate*. The domain is separated from the city of Lourdes by a tall wrought-iron fence. When they passed through St. Joseph's Gate, in Pete's words, "It was as if you left the world behind. This was holy ground."

The Basilica of the Immaculate Conception dominates the area because it sits directly above the grotto—some fifty feet above the Rosary Plaza, the grotto, and the rest of the domain.

As they walked along the basilica adjacent to the river, a

gentle breeze brought the sound of French, German, and other European languages from those around them. Just past the church, they discovered the exposed rock face that formed the grotto where Mary appeared to Bernadette. A statue of Mary was placed in the natural recess of the rough rock face where Mary had actually stood in 1858. A large altar had been placed just under the large rock overhang. Multiple three-foot-tall candles were arranged on a metal frame that rose up to a height of twelve feet in the shape of a Christmas tree—wider at the bottom, tapering to a single candle at the top.

It was hard to imagine the scene when Mary first appeared to Bernadette, because so much had changed—to imagine that the Mother of God appeared to a fourteen-year-old girl at this very spot was amazing. They stood silently gazing up to the statue of Mary. It was a very holy place. Pete recalled, "There is a sense there that you can't explain. You are in awe. Seeing the grotto with the statue of the Virgin Mary in that setting— it gives you goose bumps."

After visiting the grotto, Barbara, Pete, and the Carnazzos decided to sit at the grotto on the benches that were placed there for the many Masses that took place every day. It was so peaceful. They talked about the highlights of their Paris visit, the train trip, and their excitement to just finally be there—at the grotto where Mary appeared to Bernadette more than 150 years earlier.

The following day they explored the lower church, called the

Rosary Basilica, which was completed in 1901. It was here at one of the many side altars that Fr. Jerry celebrated Mass for their group of pilgrims. It was the Eucharist that they shared, so far from California that united them. After communion, they knelt in silence. Each one spoke to God with his or her personal needs and thanksgiving. It was so peaceful!

After Mass, they proceeded to *the baths* to experience the miraculous water of the spring. The lines were very long, with the men waiting in one covered area and the women in another. They sat apprehensively on benches with other pilgrims while they all waited their turn. Their reason for being there was different from Barbara's. They were not sick, like Barbara, but yet they wanted to experience the baths too.

Before long Jerry and Pete were separated. Pete was escorted into a curtained cubicle adjacent to the enclosed bath, while Jerry went in another. Pete undressed except for a wrap that he was given. Once he was ready, he was led to the bath. The bath is about eight feet long, formed in the concrete floor with steps leading down one end, with a colored ceramic frieze of Mary on the opposite wall. Pete sat momentarily in the water with the help of two men volunteers. "The water was the coldest water I have ever experienced! The interesting part was that when I got out of the water, I looked for a towel...and I am [already] dry. I mean physically dry." Pete said that he walked from the tub to his clothes and looked around and thought, "What's going on?" Later, Pete said to Jerry, "When you got out of the water..." but before he could finish, Jerry said, "I was completely dry!" Pete responded, "Me too!"

Nearly two years after their arrival back home, the cancer returned. This time the prognosis was not good. Barbara was back at CHOMP. Months later, one of the nurses relayed to Pete what she had heard at Mass that morning, when Fr. Jerry spoke about Barbara. "A friend of mine is in her final stages of life. I went to the hospital to be of help to her—when in fact she was ministering to me. She said, 'Fr. Jerry, this is in God's hands. We can't change it. I have had a good sixty-seven years. I am ready to go home to be with God.'" Barbara had not been *cured* at Lourdes, but she was *healed*—given the grace to accept death without fear.

In the last weeks of her life, unknown to Pete, Barbara made all the arrangements for her upcoming funeral Mass, from who was to do the readings that she had chosen, to the selection of songs to be sung. Fr. Mike Miller, her pastor at Sacred Heart Church in Salinas, had carefully taken notes of Barbara's choices. Looking back on it now, the second verse of the song that she chose seems so appropriate because it truly reflected Barbara's attitude about her coming death.

"BE NOT AFRAID"

If you pass through raging waters in the sea,
you shall not drown.
If you walk amid the burning flames,
you shall not be harmed.
If you stand before the power of hell
and death is at your side,
know that I am with you through it all.
Be not afraid. I go before you always.
Come follow me and I will give you rest.

BOB DUFFORD, S.J.

———•———

¹ The Miraculous Medal was revealed to St. Catherine Labouré with Mary acting as the *life-size model* of the image on the medal. On the front of the medal, Mary is standing on a globe, which represents the world, with her hands extended at her side. The date 1830 is below Mary's feet on the globe. The words "O Mary, conceived without sin, pray for us who have recourse to Thee" are inscribed on the perimeter of the medal.

On the other side, in the center is a cross linked to the letter M. Below each leg of the M are the images of the heart of Jesus wrapped in a crown of thorns and the heart of Mary pierced by a sword. There are twelve stars surrounding the perimeter. By the time of St. Catherine's death, more than one billion medals had been distributed.

St. Catherine died in 1876, and her body was exhumed fifty-six years later and was found to be incorrupt. "Her eyes are as blue as the day she died."

Her body can be seen in a glass coffin at the front of the Chapel at Rue de Bac. Her hands are held in prayerful repose holding a rosary. She appears to be asleep with no sign of decay

[2] There were a total of eighteen apparitions beginning on February 11, 1858, and ending on July 16, 1858. The story of Bernadette is well documented in the 2008 book *Wonders of Lourdes* and in the classic 1943 movie *The Song of Bernadette*, which still can be viewed on the Internet.

At the request of Bernadette's parish priest, Bernadette asked the beautiful lady who she was. When Mary responded, "I am the Immaculate Conception," Bernadette had no idea what that meant, since the term was beyond her fourteen years of age, and the term had not yet been circulated throughout the world.

It seems clear that Our Lady wanted her Immaculate Conception to be well known. Both in Paris in 1830 and Lourdes in 1858, Mary identified herself in similar terms: "Mary, conceived without sin, pray for us," and at Lourdes as the "Immaculate Conception."

The Catechism of the Catholic Church defines the dogma of the Immaculate Conception in this way: "That from the first moment of her conception, Mary—by the singular grace of God and by virtue of the merits of Jesus Christ—was preserved immune from original sin" (*CCC Glossary*, p. 883).

CHAPTER 18

Our Encounter

———◆———

Story from Tom Lukes from St. Joseph's Catholic Church in Spreckels, California, and Sacred Heart Army Chapel in Seaside, California.

I give you a new commandment: love one another. As I have loved you, so you also should love one another. This is how all will know that you are my disciples, if you have love for one another.

JOHN 13:34–35

WHEN OUR TWO SONS WERE ages five and three, my sister, Terry, and my brother-in-law, Duane, attended a Marriage Encounter[1] weekend. They were so enthusiastic about it that they wanted my wife, Lois, and me to go as well. When we asked them to tell us more about it, they asked us to attend an upcoming *information dinner* for people who were interested in attending a weekend. We reluctantly agreed to attend.

I remember thinking that we had a great marriage. We didn't need any help, and besides I was afraid that I would have to stand up and say something to the group in the course of the weekend. I thought that by going to the information dinner, I could satisfy my sister and brother-in-law. In the back of my mind, I was sure I could find an excuse not to attend.

As it turned out, the dinner was in a private residence and was very enjoyable. There were about six couples in attendance. Everyone seemed to be very friendly, but I learned very little about what I could expect on the Marriage Encounter weekend.

Terry and Duane seemed to think that now that we had attended the information dinner, we should be ready to sign up. I really wanted to say *yes* to please my sister, so I asked Duane, "Can you tell me more about what takes place on the weekend?" To this day, I still remember Duane's response. He said, "Tom, you're just going to have to trust me on this." I realized immediately that *he had me*. If I said I didn't want to go, it would a clear statement that I did not trust him. So I gave in and said that we would go.

I still remember driving to a hotel in Los Angeles near the airport where the Marriage Encounter weekend was to take place, wondering, *What have I gotten myself into?* Lois was fine with it because she saw it as a weekend together away from the kids. On the other hand, I anticipated the worst weekend of my life! I kept thinking our marriage doesn't need help. We have a fine marriage. Why didn't I just tell

Duane *no?* As we pulled into the motel parking lot, I real-ized it was too late.

Like Duane, I cannot reveal too much about what happened on the weekend, except to say that several couples took turns sharing very meaningful parts of their journey as husband and wife. A priest was part of the team, and he sat up at the table with them. Later, his talk helped me understand the sacrament of marriage in a new light—marriage as a *trinity*: God, the husband and the wife. You need to have God as part of the marriage for true happiness and success.

I never had to talk to the group, but we did eat family style, with four couples per table. This gave us a chance to interact with other couples. A good part of the weekend was just special private time for Lois and me alone in our hotel room following the program of the Marriage Encounter weekend.

We arrived Friday night and left Sunday afternoon after the closing Mass. Something happened in those few days that I still cannot explain. I can say that when we drove home on that June afternoon, we felt like we were returning from our honeymoon. We had found the original spark in our marriage that we had not even realized had gradually faded away.

During this short period, I also discovered that over the seven years of marriage, we had begun to take each other for granted in little ways—especially me. For instance, I no longer opened the car door for Lois when we were together like I had done when we dated, and I didn't help Lois with the dishes any longer—just to mention a few things.

Marriage Encounter helped us rekindle the romance in our marriage. But, I also have to say that, besides a great blessing to our marriage, three things occurred as a result of that weekend that changed my life forever.

First of all, we discovered that *priests were people too*! What I mean is simply that we had always set priests up on a pedestal, and for this reason we only interacted with them in a very formal way. We never had thought about inviting one of them over for dinner, asking him about his own family, or asking him what led him to the priesthood.

From that day forward, we realized that not only could we befriend our parish priest, but we also realized that all *our priests needed our friendship*. I should stress that this was not part of the weekend teaching. It was simply a result of hearing the priest talk to us in a place outside church.

Secondly, *the Mass came alive for us*. The Eucharist had new meaning. We started coming a little early on Sunday. We discovered that we felt much more part of the Mass by sitting up near the front, where we could see better what was going on. It helped our young boys' behavior as well, because they could see the priest and altar servers.

It was as if a door had opened to the church, and we had

discovered the great beauty that was inside. I was so proud to be Catholic. I actually looked forward to going to Mass. I should point out this had to be a special blessing from God that had nothing to do with the Marriage Encounter weekend, but it does seem to be a natural result that most people experience.

Finally, the most unusual gift of the weekend experience was *love*. I found that all of a sudden, I loved everyone I encountered. It was unique to me. Lois, Terry, and Duane did not experience it. This was something that God wanted to show me that I sorely needed in my life. God wanted me to love my fellow man, even the one who cut me off on the freeway.

I still remember an individual that I had to work with at a jobsite whom I could not stand. In fact, I must admit that in the past, I had spoken badly of him to my partner. However, on the Tuesday following the weekend, I attended a site meeting in which he was also present. I found that I actually had to hold back from giving him a hug. I couldn't explain this. I felt as if he were my brother. This experience of intense love for all mankind that I experienced lasted about two weeks. But even when the intensity lessened, I was still a different person because of it.

It wasn't until twenty years later that I think I found an explanation of what had happened to me. A woman from my parish had also experienced the same overwhelming love as I had. It too had been intense for about two weeks, but it was not initiated by a Marriage Encounter weekend. She explained that she had experienced the love that God has for all of us. She said that she saw everyone through the eyes of Jesus.

This explanation fit into what I had experienced as well, because it did not matter what the individual had said to me in the past or even if I didn't know him at all. I felt an overwhelming love for him. I thought about Jesus's teaching in the New Testament.

In the parable of the Prodigal Son, God is represented by the father, waiting for his lost son to return in order to embrace him and welcome him back into the family. "While he was still a long way off, his father caught sight of him, and was filled with compassion. He ran to his son, embraced him and kissed him." (Lk 15:20). All the son had to do was *come home* and *seek forgiveness.* God loves us just like any father loves his children, even when they have done something wrong. He is just waiting for our return home.

It is remarkable what happens when we are willing to *yield to God* and allow Him to show us how to live our lives to the fullness that God had always intended.

---

[1] "A *Marriage Encounter* is a Catholic process that married couples *of all faiths* can experience over a two-day weekend. The weekend gives spouses an opportunity to grow in their marriage through open and honest communication, face-to-face sharing, and heart-to-heart encounter in a comfortable, relaxed setting. *Marriage Encounter* invites and encourages married couples

of all ages and faith expressions to share in this experience and to become an integral part of this journey" (National Marriage Encounter website, http://marriage-encounter.org/). See also the chapter 30 entitled "Baptism of Fire."

CHAPTER 19

The Challenge

———————

Story from Clem Richardson from St. Joseph's Catholic Church in Spreckels, California

> *You have made us for yourself, O Lord, and our heart is restless until it rests in you.*

St. Augustine's Confessions

It was a cool February afternoon as Clem and Ken approached the old San Antonio Mission near King City. Clem had reluctantly agreed to attend a CIC[1] (Christians in Commerce) Challenge Weekend. Little did he know the significance that this retreat would have on the rest of his life.

As he carried his bag from the car to the mission, Clem asked himself how he had ended up at this retreat weekend. He remembered that it was some months earlier that Clem had asked his former high school friend Ken to donate an auction item for the annual Palma–Notre Dame Auction. (The auction was the major fundraiser for the two Catholic High Schools in Salinas.) Ken responded by donating a video game that raised more than $700.

Later, when Ken asked him to attend a CIC Weekend, Clem felt he had to say *yes* in response to Ken's earlier generosity. Before the auction, Clem had turned down Ken on other occasions because the CIC Weekend meant giving up an entire weekend of his life. His weekends were important to him; it was a chance to play golf and just relax. He didn't need to go on a retreat. He went to church every Sunday—even his wife, Barbara, said he was a good Christian—and what about his good deeds, like being in charge of the auction? If someone said he was "a lukewarm Catholic," he could always point to someone who was worse.

Clem explained that his philosophy back then was that of a *Christian accountant*. He rationalized it this way: "If I make three good choices and two bad ones, I am still in the plus." This thinking would soon be challenged, because CIC was very much about committing your life to God totally, not just partway.

It was to this old mission building that Clem found himself approaching on that late afternoon in February. Ken made a point to ask Clem to think of something specific that he would like to have God change in his life on this retreat. This could serve as a goal for the retreat. It didn't take Clem long to come up with two goals, which he kept to himself. Now they were ready to enter the mission grounds to unload their bags in their assigned rooms.

The retreat started Friday and concluded Sunday afternoon. The group attending the retreat was made up of men who had made the retreat before and men who were making it for the first time. The format of the retreat was a series of talks to provide the tools to live a Christ-filled life. The team members had all made the retreat before and were living the life that CIC was promoting.

Those in attendance were soon divided into small groups. After each talk the groups would get together to discuss the talk and share how the talks impacted or applied to their lives. Clem enjoyed the guys in his group, especially the wisdom that some shared from their own lives.

There was a point on Saturday when the individuals in the groups were *prayed over* for their particular needs and to receive the Holy Spirit. Clem really expected to experience something special. While he was being prayed over, he asked God to help him with his two goals for the weekend—things he wanted to change in his life. He expected to feel something, but he felt nothing extraordinary.

The rest of Saturday flew by. That night there was a special dinner. They all put on coats and ties to share *the Lord's Supper*, which was a special CIC traditional Saturday dinner. The food was great, and he liked singing Christian songs from the notebook that each participant was given. He went to bed happy that he had come. He realized that the talks really challenged him to change. He was beginning to understand why this retreat was called a "challenge weekend." Clem wondered if he could follow through on the call he was hearing to go *all in* for Jesus.

Sunday morning started with Mass in the mission church which both the Catholics and non-Catholics attended, followed by a great breakfast. After a short break, all the men gathered again in the meeting room to hear more talks.

Clem was in a struggle of wills—his will and God's. All day, he could not pay attention to the talks. His real focus was his battle with his Christian accounting rule. Why did God need him to commit to making all five good choices in his life? What was wrong with three of five? He remembered that Jesus said: "You therefore, must be perfect, as your heavenly Father is perfect" (Mt 5:48). Clem knew that if he committed to what CIC asked of him and what he felt God wanted, it would affect all areas of his life—daily prayer, living by the golden rule, scripture study, and so on. This presented a real challenge for Clem. Was he ready for this?

He even worried that he might lose his job if he accepted the challenge. He knew that the produce industry, especially sales, could be rough. He was supposed to be a tough guy working for the best price for the firm. Could he still work in sales as a fired-up Christian? He wanted to change—but at what cost? He wanted to be like the guys who had spoken of their *personal relationship* with Christ. He wanted that, but was he willing to make the commitment?

Later Sunday morning, it all came to a head. He knew what he had to do. He concluded, "I've been a fool for just about everything else in life, why not try being a fool for Jesus?" He let God know that he was willing to turn his life over to Him. God would be first, then his family, and finally work and everything else. When he finally made this commitment, his spirit was filled with *rejoicing*. Something had finally happened! Clem believed it was the ancestors of his family buried there at the mission whose prayers had finally been answered.

He returned home that night fired up. He made a decision to get started the very next morning by setting time aside for prayer. He wanted to develop that *personal relationship* with Christ, and it all had to start with prayer. Then he would begin to read the Bible seriously for the first time.

Some people at work immediately noticed the change. "What are you so happy about?" His fear of losing his job never materialized. He was eventually moved out of sales and into the processing and product development arm of the company. This turned out to be where Clem felt he belonged, where God wanted him all along.

Today, twenty-eight years later, Clem shared that after the CIC Weekend, *both* his goals were answered, but more importantly, Clem feels closer to God. God is no longer distant; now Clem feels he can just talk with God as he would talk to his best friend. The CIC Weekend changed Clem's life forever. He now has a *personal relationship* with Christ!

———•———

[1] CIC was founded in the early 1980s. Fr. Michael Scanlan, the former president of Franciscan University in Steubenville, Ohio, was asked by several businessmen to help them put together a retreat weekend to help Christian men be strengthened in their faith. They wanted this retreat to transform lives through the Holy Spirit, to bring his love and presence to the workplace. CIC is for all Christian men, not just Catholics.

CHAPTER 20

The Cross

———•———

Story from Clem Richardson from St. Joseph's Catholic
Church in Spreckels, California

> *The message of the cross is foolishness to those who are perishing,*
> *but to us who are being saved it is the power of God.*

1 CORINTHIANS 1:18

FOUR YEARS AFTER MAKING HIS CIC Weekend, Clem was
back at San Antonio Mission. This time, he was part of
the CIC team. It was Saturday night. Looking over his talk on
service, he began to wonder if he shouldn't make some changes
to build on some of the talks given earlier on Saturday. His
talk wasn't until Sunday, so he had some time.

He tried to think of a person who really exhibited the traits
of service to use as an example in his talk. Immediately, he
thought of his mother, Georgia. Why not? The other men
could relate to their mothers too. Reflecting on how much his

mom had exemplified service in his early life and still continued to this day, he decided to let her know of his gratitude once this retreat weekend was over.

The following Monday, Clem met his mom in her kitchen. He looked at her tenderly and told her that he loved her and appreciated all she had done for him in his life. No doubt surprised, she was quick to respond with love in return. A loving hug followed. Clem resolved that it should not end there. From then on, whenever he came into contact with his mom, he would express his love and give her a hug.

Her love for Clem was an *agape* kind of love, as Fr. Tom Hall said recently during his Mother's Day homily. A mother's love is self-giving, sacrificing always. That could be seen in accepting the pain of childbirth not just the first time but knowing the pain that she will have to face, accepting it the second, third, and in Clem's case, a fourth time. That is true *agape love!*

On August 15 of that year, the oldest daughter of Clem's cousin was getting married in a Catholic church in San Jose, so Clem packed up the family to make the hour drive north to the church. Barbara and Clem dropped the children off at a nearby amusement park on the way, and proceeded to the church, where they sat in front of his mom and dad to witness the wedding. At the sign of peace, Clem greeted his dad and told his mom again that he loved her, followed by the now-usual hug.

Soon the wedding Mass was over, and everyone was heading

to the reception at La Rinconada Country Club in Los Gatos. The reception gave Clem and Barbara a chance to visit with friends and family and enjoy a great meal. Soon it was time to head home. As they were heading for their car, standing in front of the country club, there was Clem's mom, Georgia, with her video camera, wanting to create another family memory.

She acted almost like a TV reporter, interviewing her son and daughter-in-law. She asked about Clem's and Barbara's recollection of their own wedding reception, which had also taken place at this same country club some years earlier. It was all in fun. It was a chance to reflect on a time long ago and spend a special moment with Clem's mom. It was dusk. The hills were golden as the sun was saying farewell to another day.

They all needed to get started driving home. Clem's mom, dad, and aunt went in one car; Clem and Barbara were in another. After picking up the children at the amusement park, Clem headed home in near silence, since it had been a full day for everyone. The kids were soon asleep.

On the way home, just past Morgan Hill, they passed a wreck on the side of the road. By then all they wanted to do was get home and get to bed, so they hardly noticed. It was already after 10:30 when they arrived home. The minute they got home, Clem received a call from Stanford Hospital. "There has been an accident. Your dad is here. We want you to come up to the hospital. Your aunt has been sent to the Trauma Center in San Jose."

Clem replied, "There were three people in the car, but you didn't mention my mom."

The response was "We try not to give this news over the phone, but since we want a family member to give that message to your dad, we need to tell you that your mom passed away in that wreck."

Clem was shocked! He had just spent the day with his mom and dad. How could this be? He immediately flashed back to the wreck they had passed on the way home. It must have been his mom's car. He had been right there! How could he not have recognized the car? Perhaps this was meant to be—a way that God might have protected them. If he had stopped, there would have been nothing he could have done, and he and the family would have to deal with that image for the rest of their lives.

It was near midnight when Clem and Barbara headed north to Stanford Hospital to check on his dad and break the news. There was silence in the car and darkness outside. Fortunately, there were very few cars on the freeway.

Clem couldn't help but ask, "God, I thought I had developed a relationship with you. What's this all about? I have been doing what you asked me to do. Why am I going through this now?" The answer was immediate: "What do you think I have been preparing you for?" This response was of some consolation, and "a moment of growth." He still had to face telling his dad the bad news.

It was late when they arrived at the hospital. Fortunately, Clem's dad was not seriously injured. He would be released the following day. Clem's news to his dad must have been devastating. It was almost as hard to tell his dad that his wife was dead as it was for Clem to hear it the first time. Clem had not only his own grief but also his fatigue to deal with. It was nearly 3:00 a.m. when they got into bed at a nearby hotel. As exhausted as Clem was, sleep would not come. Finally, as dawn approached, Clem again cried out to God, "Why did this have to happen?"

Just as Clem posed the question to God, dawn broke, and with it a shadow was cast onto the high ceiling. The shadow was in the form of a cross. Clem prayerfully asked if this was a sign from God, and if so, what was His message? The answer came: "I have power over everything—all life, death and creation—and yet I chose to die on the cross. If I chose this death, surely you understand that death is inevitable."

More than twenty years later, Clem still recalls the comfort that the shadow of the cross brought him on that morning and the words that accompanied it in his mind. He was so grateful that he had those many opportunities to express his love to his mom before she died. He realized that so many people regret that they never shared their feelings with a loved one, and then it is too late.

Clem's final thought was this: "It is really apparent, when you have a relationship with God through Jesus, that there will still be troubles. When the troubles are the worst, if you are looking, He is the closest."

CHAPTER 21

Finding St. Anthony

—◆—

Story from Tom Lukes from St. Joseph's Catholic Church in Spreckels, California, and Sacred Heart Army Chapel in Seaside, California.

> *The intercession of the saints. "Being more closely united to*
> *Christ, those who dwell in heaven fix the whole Church more*
> *firmly in holiness…They do not cease to intercede with the Father*
> *for us, as they proffer the merits which they acquired on earth*
> *through the one mediator between God and men, Christ Jesus…*
> *So by their fraternal concern is our weakness greatly helped."*

1 TIMOTHY 2:5; CATECHISM OF THE CATHOLIC CHURCH, 956

I GREW UP GOING TO CATHOLIC schools in the Washington DC area, where my first understanding of saints was from the examples shown in the actual lives of the nuns who taught me at Blessed Sacrament School and later in high school by the Benedictine monks who taught me at St. Anselm's Priory.

In fifth grade, Sister Bernadine was someone I especially looked up to as a true saint in my life. *She was special.* One of the things she taught us that I still remember was that before we criticize someone else, we should first look at ourselves. Her beauty reminded me of Ingrid Bergman when she played St. Joan of Arc in a movie that also influenced my life. The stories of saints were also taught to us as examples of people we could emulate.

Later in my life, I discovered that the saints could be approached in prayer for *help* and *assistance.* As an example, I began to turn to prayer to St. Anthony for help in finding things that I had misplaced or lost. I must admit I only turn to St. Anthony when all else fails.

The patron saint of lost things was a contemporary of St. Francis of Assisi. He was most famous for his preaching. In fact, when his tomb was examined for his cause of sainthood, it was discovered that his entire body had turned to dust except his tongue, which had been preserved. St. Anthony died in 1231 at the age of thirty-six. This Internet story on St. Anthony explains why he is the saint of lost things:

> *The story is that a novice carried off a valuable book of psalms that St. Anthony was using. St. Anthony prayed very hard that the psalter would be found. After seeing an alarming apparition of St. Anthony, the novice returned the psalter. A little jingle goes like this: "St. Anthony, please look around; something is lost and must be found."*

Here are a few examples of how St. Anthony of Padua has an-swered my prayers:

My first example of how St. Anthony helps came last summer when my wife, son Stephen, and I traveled to Paris. One rainy Sunday after Mass at Notre Dame Cathedral, we decided to take the Metro and go to the Louvre. That day the Metro was packed shoulder to shoulder because it was the first Sunday of the month, which meant that tickets to enter the Louvre were free. As we departed the Metro at the Louvre entrance, I instinctively checked my back pocket for my wallet. *It was gone.*

We had heard many stories of pickpockets in Paris. For that reason, I had been keeping my wallet in my front pocket, but that Sunday I must have forgotten and gone back to my old ways, putting the wallet in my back pocket.

I could not remember anyone bumping into me, so I wanted to believe that it wasn't a pickpocket. I thought maybe I had left it at the little restaurant where we had enjoyed lunch before getting on the Metro. So I returned to the Metro and retraced my route back to the restaurant. As I stood inside that Metro car with my heart pounding, I began to imagine how much cash the thief would be able to withdraw before we canceled the credit cards. About this time, I called on St. Anthony in prayer. I asked St. Anthony to help me find the wallet.

When I arrived at the restaurant and spoke to the owner, he said that he had not seen my wallet, and a quick search of our table revealed nothing. I was actually not surprised. I was sure that I had my wallet when I left the restaurant, but I just could not imagine how someone was able to take it without my being aware of it happening. As I headed back to the Louvre on the Metro, it dawned on me that this was the first time St. Anthony had let me down. At this point, I had more important things on my mind, like how quickly we could return to our hotel and report my credit cards stolen.

By the time I returned to the Louvre and met my waiting wife and son, a full hour had passed. We headed back to the hotel, very conscious of the time passing. The hotel concierge was very helpful, and the cards were quickly canceled. That night after dinner, I checked my e-mail on the Internet and found a message from my office in Salinas saying that a woman in Paris had found my wallet. She had used information in my wallet to reach work. I later discovered that the thief had apparently taken only the cash and had tossed the wallet into the gutter on a narrow out-of-the-way side street. All the credit cards and my driver's license were still there.

When Lois and I sat at dinner that night, I learned that she too had prayed to St. Anthony while I was racing back to the restaurant. She pointed out that St. Anthony had not let us down after all; we *had* found the wallet. I suggested that next time we needed to be more specific and ask St. Anthony to help us find not just the wallet but also the money.

My second example came only as I began to trust St. Anthony's help. You see, as I have gotten older, I have had trouble remembering the names of people. I found myself very frustrated, but I decided that if St. Anthony could help me find lost items, he could also help me find lost names. Just now, it happened again. I wanted to remember the actress who played Joan of Arc earlier in this story. For the life of me, I could not think of her name, so I asked St. Anthony to help and the name, Ingrid Bergman, immediately popped into my head.

The third example of St. Anthony's help again involved a missing wallet. I should mention that before I start a round of golf, I normally take my keys and wallet and place them in my golf bag to make room for golf balls, tees, and ball marker in my pockets.

My seventeen-year-old son, Stephen, and I were playing golf at Rancho Canada in Carmel Valley. As it turned out, darkness caught us in the middle of the ninth fairway, so we simply picked up our balls and walked in from there, talking as we walked. By the time we walked back to the car, there was barely any light left. I dug into the pocket of my golf bag and immediately found the car keys, but no wallet. A quick search revealed that *the wallet was gone.*

I realized that the chances of returning in the dark to find the wallet were remote, especially since the wallet could have fallen out of the golf bag anywhere on the front nine holes. I knew that even if it were found the next morning, it would probably be missing all my credit cards or the lawn sprinklers that go off during the night would have ruined it.

As soon as we loaded the golf clubs in the car, Steve and I set off to retrace our steps. Starting at the car and walking back up the ninth fairway toward the ninth green, we began searching in the ever-growing darkness. We attempted to walk back along the same way we had come earlier, but we were competing with time. I thought, if only I had *a flashlight*!

Even as we searched, I began wondering what I would do if I were unable to find the wallet. I was thinking about returning at dawn the next morning to look again. I realized the odds of finding the wallet that night were remote. It could be anywhere. By the time we reached the eighth green, we could barely see. I said to my son, "It's time to pray to St. Anthony for help." So I held Stephen's hand, right there on the eighth green, and I prayed out loud to St. Anthony, asking for help.

We walked off that green heading toward the cart path no more than twenty paces—and there on the ground was a dark form. I moved it with my foot to make sure it wasn't something alive; I then bent over and picked it up. It was my wallet! The time elapsed from my prayer to St. Anthony and finding the wallet was less than forty-five seconds, and this time the money was still in the wallet!

Thank you, St. Anthony!

CHAPTER 22

High School Blues

———◆———

Story from Kathleen Hicks from Sacred Heart Catholic Church in Salinas, California

> *Since you have purified yourselves by obedience to the truth for*
> *sincere mutual, love one another intensely from a [pure] heart.*
> *You have been born anew, not from a perishable seed, through*
> *the living and abiding word of God, for: "All flesh is like grass,*
> *and all its glory like the flower of the field; the grass withers, and*
> *the flower wilts; but the word of the Lord remains forever."*

1 PETER 1:22–23

S HE SAT ALONE, HIDING IN the safest place she could find, the school library at Mercy Catholic High School. The *no talking* rule was what made it her *safe house*. Here, she could work on her homework, avoiding eye contact with everyone, and not worry about talking to anyone.

Kathy described herself, as "very shy and pretty overweight, with pimples." She did have a couple of friends, who were also shy, quiet types. Thus far, high school had not been a great experience. If only she felt better about herself and had some friends, life would be so much better.

Kathy walked with her head down between classes, trying not to be noticed. School had become a place where she would rather not be. But school wasn't all bad. She could point to her success in her studies as the best part of high school, but her low self-esteem contributed to her shyness and lack of friends.

She recalls that in sixth through eighth grade, her faith was lacking. It was a matter of "following the rules and doing what the nuns told me." In high school, she really didn't think much about God. He was a distant figure she could not relate to, especially since her main focus was just to make it through the day.

No doubt, Kathy's shyness was apparent to her teachers. This would explain why her religion teacher, Sister Jeanne Marie, approached her one day in her junior year to suggest that she should consider attending the upcoming retreat. Kathy had no idea what a retreat was, but Sister explained that it was a time away from home and school to grow closer to God.

Kathy became apprehensive. It might be a time to grow closer to God, but it also might force her to talk with the other people on the retreat. This was her immediate concern, until Sister Jeanne Marie said the magic word: it was to be a *silent* retreat. That did not sound so bad after all. With her family's blessing, she decided to go.

The retreat was held at the Santa Sabina Retreat House at Dominican College in San Rafael. The campus was beautiful, but Kathy had a lot of things on her mind. Even before she arrived at her room, questions began to flood her mind. She was really hoping that this retreat would help her grow closer to God, but she was filled with doubt. It all started with the question, "Where was God in my life?" She wasn't really sure about God. She thought, "I don't even know that there is a God out there."

Based on her high school experiences, she felt that if there were a God, where had he been during her struggles? She wasn't feeling good about herself. She didn't have many friends and she couldn't even talk with people at all. Her belief in God was based entirely on being obedient, following the rules, and not questioning anything about God. She was attending a Catholic high school, so no one ever debated that God exists. It was just assumed that He did.

She had been raised Catholic by Catholic parents. She had nearly eleven years of Catholic education, but now she began to have doubts. "Is God real, and if so, where has He been? My life has been so miserable!" But now that she was at the retreat, she decided to just follow directions and hope for the best. That's all she could do anyway. Perhaps this retreat would help her to discover God in a new way like Sister Jeanne Marie had said. She hoped so!

After finding her room and settling in, Kathy attended a large group presentation. The priest leading the retreat set the format and ground rules of the weekend retreat, but with it came a new problem for Kathy. He announced that each person would have to meet *one-on-one* with an assigned seminarian. Kathy's first thought was: "I thought that this was supposed to be a *silent* retreat!"

Those participating in the retreat were to go immediately to meet with their assigned seminarian to receive individual direction. Terrified and shaking, with her head down, she entered the room where she was to meet her assigned seminarian. "I couldn't say anything to him at all." It must have been immediately obvious to the seminarian that Kathy was frightened. He needed to take a new approach. He directed Kathy, "Go to the chapel and take your Bible. Just open it, and see what it says."

She wasn't sure why she needed to do this. Right now, she was still dealing with the basic question of whether there even was a God. But the seminarian had told her to do it, so she gladly escaped and obediently went to the chapel and opened the Bible. Her eyes immediately went to 1 John 4:7–8, which reads, "Beloved, let us love one another, because love is of God; everyone who loves is begotten of God and knows God. Whoever is without love does not know God, for God is love."

Kathy said, "It felt like God was talking to me right then!" She realized that she did not love anyone at school because she was afraid to talk with anyone, except for those few *shy, quiet types* like herself. She also realized that *knowing God* was tied to *loving others*. This meant that she would have to change. Kathy was really excited. "God just spoke to me! I need to come out of myself, because He said that's how I will know Him...*by loving others*."

Before she left the chapel, she became aware of the beautiful stained glass windows in the chapel. She had been so focused on herself and her struggle that she had not even noticed them. They were beautiful, filling the chapel with colored light. One of the windows portrayed a black saint. In the bottom corner of his stained glass window was pictured a little *white mouse*. She wondered who this black saint was, and why was there a white mouse in the stained glass window. What did that mean? (Kathy later discovered that the black saint's name was St. Martin de Porres.[1])

She left the chapel excited, so she decided to take a walk in the garden. It was there that she came across another surprise. There, lying in the leaves in the garden was a dead *white mouse*. "God is really trying to get my attention," Kathy said to herself. She didn't know what all this meant, but after the retreat was over, she would have to find out.

When she returned to Mercy Catholic High School, she went to the library—this time not as a safe house but as a source of information. She found out that St. Martin de Porres was a Dominican brother.

This experience at the silent retreat greatly changed Kathy's life. Afterward, her whole attitude changed. She now knew that God was real. *He was love itself.* She now had a reason to come out of her shell and learn to love others—so she could *know God.* It would not be easy, but now she had a purpose.

NOTE: Kathy felt God had called her attention to St. Martin de Porres for a reason. She learned that he was known for his care for the sick and he founded a children's hospital. This inspired Kathy to direct her life to working with children with disabilities. She went on to receive a Masters in Special Education and now works for the Monterey County Office of Education at a special-day class for children with orthopedic handicaps.

---

[1] St. Martin lived in Peru from 1579 to 1639. He was especially known for his love of the poor and needy. He established a children's hospital. He is often pictured with a white mouse because of the following story about St. Martin:

One time there seemed to be a mouse "convention" in the wardrobe room of the monastery, where they feasted on the finest linen garments and sheets, leaving the old ones untouched. Some of the monks wanted to poison the rodents, but Martin would not hear of it. One day he caught a little mouse and held him gently, and said, "Little brother, why are you and your companions doing so much harm to the things belonging to the sick? Look; I shall not kill you, but you are to assemble all your friends and lead them to the far end of the garden. Every day I will bring you food if you leave the wardrobe alone." After Martin let go of the mouse, there was scurrying from every nook and cranny, and the procession started toward the monastery garden. Martin, tall and slender, with long strides, led the mice to their new home. Every day he brought them a meal, and no mouse ever set claw or tooth in the monastery wardrobe.

(source http://www.martindeporres.org/about.htm)

CHAPTER 23

The Old Car

Story from Tom Lukes from St. Joseph's Catholic Church in Spreckels, California, and Sacred Heart Army Chapel in Seaside, California.

Rejoice in hope, endure in afflictions, persevere in prayer.

ROMANS 12:12

IT WAS A BRIGHT, SUNNY Friday morning, as I drove up Carmel Valley Road. I had an appointment with a new client, Mr. and Mrs. Parker, who wanted to hire us to do an addition to a house that my architectural firm had designed more than fifteen years earlier, well before I was a part of the firm. I had seen pictures of the house that was in the Quail Lodge development. It was a real *award winner*! I was looking forward to be involved with the new addition.

Perhaps it was because of my admiration for the great design that I felt apprehensive about being the architect assigned to do the design of the addition. But the apprehension only increased when I had to deal with *where to park.*

As I viewed the house for the first time from the street, I could see that the house had been carefully sited among the oak trees along the ridgeline overlooking distant hills. I considered using the short, circular drive to park right in front of the large double front door. *I hesitated.*

I was driving a brown Toyota Celica that was at least fifteen years old. The car was paid for, but we were struggling to just pay the regular bills, so I had to live with driving an old car. I wanted to make a good impression with the new client, and parking my old car in front of their front door would not serve that purpose. I quickly made a U-turn to position my car just out of sight down the street from the front door. I then walked up to the house to meet the new clients.

Unfortunately, after greeting me, Mrs. Parker's first question was, "Where did you park your car?" I was *caught.* I was forced to explain my motive for parking my car out of sight from the front door. I explained I was driving a rather old car that I was not comfortable parking in front of their home.

Mr. Parker said that that was a good sign that our firm would not be overcharging them for the architectural work. We continued inside for our meeting. As it turned out, the addition was to be an artist's sculpture studio, complete with fireplace and outside deck. I liked Mr. and Mrs. Parker and their two young daughters. It was going to be an exciting project after all.

When the meeting was over, the Parkers insisted on walking me out to my car to have a good look at it. Perhaps they wanted to see just how bad it looked. In any event, as I drove off, I reflected on the new client and the challenge of the project that I had ahead of me, and I immediately forgot about the embarrassment of driving that old Toyota.

The weekend passed, as it usually does, much too fast. Monday, I left at 6:30 for morning Mass at Sacred Heart Church in Salinas about a half mile from work. I was about to get on highway 68, the freeway that leads to Salinas, when I had a strange command pop into my mind: "Pray for a car." I told myself, "No, that's crazy! You don't pray for cars." But again the thought returned: "Pray for a car." So I said to myself, "If God wants me to pray for a car, I will." It felt almost disrespectful doing so. I realized that I hadn't been even thinking about last Friday's encounter at the Parkers' house. The need to pray had just popped into my head out of the blue.

With the prayer finished, I was off to church, followed by a full day at work. Nothing happened with my prayer that day— no special call telling me that I had won a car, nothing! I don't know what I thought would happen, but I had prayed as I felt I had been urged to do, so I just forgot all about it. Tuesday came and went. I had completely forgotten about the urge to pray for a car.

On Wednesday night after dinner, my parents called from Southern California. I was a little concerned that something might be wrong; but they said that they just wanted to ask me if I would be interested in having their five-year-old car, since they were going to buy a new one. My immediate reaction was to tell them of my prayer on Monday morning. Mom said, "Well, we would have called Monday, but we just didn't get around to it."

CHAPTER 24

The Anointing

Story from John from St. Joseph's Catholic Church in Spreckels, California

> *But the one who gives us security with you in Christ and*
> *who anointed us is God; he has also put his seal upon us and*
> *given the Spirit in our hearts as a first installment.*

2 CORINTHIANS 1:21, 22

O FTEN WE ARE NOT AWARE of how our early childhood surroundings, friends, and circumstances influence us until years later, when we can look back and see it in perspective. "Hindsight is twenty-twenty." This was true of John's story as well.

John said that when he grew up, he had a very dysfunctional family. His father was in prison, which left his mother to raise both John and his brother on a small salary without her husband's support. They were so poor that John still remembers that for his brother's birthday, his mom took them to McDonald's for dinner. She only had enough money to pay for one hamburger that John and his brother split.

Being poor did not stop his mother from deciding to take John and his brother out of Los Padres Public School to send them to Madonna del Sasso Catholic School. At the time, John did not understand how much sacrifice this change in schools meant to his mom. Looking back on it today, he says that this move probably saved his life. If she had not sent him to a Catholic school, he would have ended up like his father—*in prison*. Or worse yet, he probably would be dead because of possible association with gangs in that public school.

So when John was ready for fourth grade and his brother for third, his mother drove them to Madonna del Sasso Catholic School for the first time. But John did not want to go. It took two teachers, a nurse, and his mother to drag him into that classroom. Over time, he accepted his mother's wish to have him receive a Catholic education. He still remembers attending Mass, school retreats, and "Covenant Camps." He also remembers clearly that it was in the seventh grade that he had his conversion experience.

It all started over a rather minor personal problem. John liked two girls, who both were cheerleaders, and he didn't know what to do about it. Their coach was Cheryl Ward-Kaiser, whom he also knew from school. He decided to seek her advice, so he asked Cheryl what he should do.

Instead of discounting the trivial nature of his problem, she said, "I can tell you what to do, but why not ask God?"

He asked her to explain.

She said what he needed to do was to take his Bible, find a quiet place, and just ask God for direction with his problem. Then, he should just open his Bible and read what God had to say.

John followed what Cheryl had suggested, but absolutely nothing happened. He called Cheryl to tell her that it didn't work. So, since *God* had not told him what to do, maybe now *she* would tell him what to do.

Cheryl reviewed with John what he had done. She said that he had not done it correctly. He had left out an important part. He had failed to believe that God would answer his prayer. She told him to do it again, but this time, *believe* that God would answer his prayer.

As a twelve-year-old, he couldn't understand why this would make any difference. But he thought to himself, I believe in God; I respect and trust Cheryl, so why not do what she suggested? So he took his Bible, and with renewed faith, he followed Cheryl's instruction. This time *something happened.*

The words he read had new meaning. He realized that the words he was reading were meant for him. The words of the Bible had *come alive* to him. The Old Testament words of Isaiah were not *old*; they were *new*. They were for him. The sense that he had made a great discovery filled him with awe for God, and he felt God's love for him. God had answered his prayer!

He could not put down the Bible. Over the weekend, he pored over the New Testament. Monday, he carried his Bible to school, where he surprised his friends when he declared that they all had to change. He and his friends could no longer be the bullies of the school. He pointed out what Jesus said about loving your neighbor. He explained that God's Word had made him want to change the way he was living. They all needed to change. From that day even until today, reading the Word of God has been his passion.

While he was still twelve, John said that he was baptized in the Holy Spirit, when he was prayed over at a prayer meeting. The experience, although only spiritual, felt so real that he felt that anyone looking at him could have seen what he was feeling over his entire body.

Although his eyes were closed, he was sure that someone was pouring warm, soothing water over his head and down over all of his body. But it was different than water. The sensation was much slower than water. Whatever it was, it was slowly cascading warmth over him, as if in slow motion.

Along with the physical sensation, John said that simultaneously he felt God's great love for him. "The feeling cannot be put into words. It engulfed me, consuming as it went—one of the most amazing things I have ever experienced. It was as if I were being *anointed*."

CHAPTER 25

The Road Less Traveled

———————

Story from Tom Lukes from St. Joseph's Catholic Church in Spreckels, California

> *Then the angel of the Lord spoke to Phillip,*
> *"Get up and head south to the road that goes down*
> *from Jerusalem to Gaza." This is a desert route.*

ACTS 8:26

W HEN I WAS THIRTY-TWO YEARS old, we moved from Pasadena to Salinas with our two young sons. We moved for a job opportunity that God had clearly provided me in Salinas, but that's another story. We soon found the St. Joseph's Catholic Church in Spreckels.

We missed our Marriage Encounter community from Pasadena,

but we soon realized that Cursillo was a strong movement in the Monterey Diocese. It helped build St. Joseph's into a loving and caring community that we soon called our own. Within five years we attended a Cursillo Weekend ourselves. I was so moved by the experience that I not only returned year after year to be part of the Cursillo team, but I soon found myself part of the *Secretariat*, the leadership of the Cursillo movement in our diocese.

At the time, the *Secretariat* met monthly in Castroville, a town some 25 minutes away from where we lived along Highway 68, outside Salinas. We met in Castroville because it was more central, especially for those coming from Santa Cruz and Monterey.

This particular night, our regular monthly meeting had gone on longer than normal. It was 10:00 p.m. when I headed home. I can remember being concerned that my wife would be worried about me. (This was before cell phones.)

My drive home always took me down Cooper Road through miles of lettuce fields. It was a very dark, lonely stretch of road that was a shortcut to get from Highway 1 to Blanco Road and eventually to my home along Highway 68.

I was about a hundred yards from the T intersection of Cooper and Blanco roads when, without any warning, the car engine and all power shut off. There was just an eerie dark silence as the car continued down the road without power.

I had thought that the narrow country road along the lettuce fields was dark before the power went off; now, without the headlights, I was in total darkness. I gripped the wheel tightly and tried to keep the car on the road by just going straight. All I could see were the lights of cars that were traveling at high speed on Blanco Road at right angles to my path but a hundred yards away. I thought, "If I could just coast close to the intersection, I could stop there, and I would be safe."

I knew I could not pull off the road onto the shoulder because much of this road had deep irrigation ditches alongside it. I could not risk going into one of those ditches because they are half full of water. As I coasted toward the intersection, I decided to try the brakes, which fortunately still worked. I coasted to a stop one car length from Blanco Road.

I knew it was useless to open up the hood of the car because I could not see anything and I did not have any idea why a car would just die like my station wagon had just done.

"What should I do now?" I asked myself. (Remember this was before cell phones!) My first thought was to find a way to call AAA to get a tow truck out to help. I decided that my best choice would be to cross Blanco Road to the single farmhouse directly opposite where I had stopped and ask to use their phone to call for help. But when I got to the other side of Blanco Road and walked up toward the front porch, I realized that the entrance stairs to the front porch, which faced the road, had been removed and boarded up. The only entrance to the house must be down the driveway, where I could hear dogs already barking.

All of a sudden, I thought that this might not be a very good idea. If the two barking dogs didn't attack me, their barking would at the very least alert the residents to my arrival, and they might be armed, just waiting to see who I was. No, this was *not* a good idea!

I looked back across the street to the dark form of my car and wondered what else I could do to get help. I first thought of hitchhiking on Blanco Road into town, but the cars, although frequent, were moving along at about sixty miles an hour, and I would be standing in the dark. No one would see me in time to risk stopping. I quickly decided that this too was also *not* a good idea.

I carefully crossed the busy road and walked back to my car. Not a single car had come along the road on which I was now parked. "Why not flag down the next car?" I thought. I realized that any car coming down Cooper would have to stop at Blanco and my car was still in the right lane of the road. They would have to stop behind my car anyway. About this time, in the distance I could see the lights of a car some half a mile away, coming down the road toward me.

All of a sudden, I realized that I was still in danger! "What if this car held someone who wanted to rob me or do me harm?" I decided that it was time to pray. "Lord God, protect me from harm. *Help me!*"

As the car came close enough to see, I was immediately filled with relief. The car was a Monterey County Sheriff's car. In all the times before or since that I have driven that road, I have never seen a sheriff's car. *God's timing was great!*

CHAPTER 26

The Healing

———•———

Story from William Kennedy, MD, from St. Joseph's Catholic Church in Salinas, California

> *Hold the physician in honor, for he is essential to you,*
> *and God it was who established his profession.*

Sir 38:1

HE WAS ONLY FIVE MINUTES away, but he knew every minute would count as he drove as quickly as possible to the ER at Salinas Memorial Hospital. His favorite patient, Margaret Edwards, was in *cardiac arrest* and would die if he couldn't find a way to save her. His quiet day off was a thing of the past. At the moment, he could only focus on making the upcoming traffic light.

It was lucky he had been home when they called from the emergency room. He just hoped it was not too late. The ER nurse said that they had been working on Margaret for nearly an hour, and they were ready to stop, when they called him as a last resort.

When he entered the emergency room, he could see the stress on the team that had responded to the *code blue*. He learned that Margaret was unconscious; she was not breathing; and her heart was in a rhythm that did not support her blood pressure.

The ER room had debris everywhere, as evidence of the frantic work that had taken place in an effort to save Margaret over the past hour.

It was not clear to him how Margaret had arrived in this condition, or if the event had occurred while being treated for chest pains, but he knew none of that mattered at the moment. It was evident that the ER team of doctors and nurses were stressed and fatigued. Dr. Kennedy was quickly briefed on what had transpired, and what they had done to save her.

While unconscious, Margaret had been assisted in breathing through a tube down her throat that was connected to a hand pump that was being operated by the respiratory therapist, while her chest was being rhythmically compressed by a nurse to help maintain her blood pressure. The ER doctor in charge reported that Margaret had received an intravenous treatment of bretylium, an antiarrhythmic agent, as well as multiple electric shocks. None of these approaches brought any response.

The atmosphere in the room was tense for this had gone on now for too long. Dr. Kennedy immediately instructed the ER staff, "Give her an injection of lidocaine, and then we can stop." He was saying to try this last drug that might save her, even though he felt that there wasn't much hope, since the ER doctor had already tried a more powerful drug in bretylium. If this didn't work, there wasn't anything else he could think of to do.

The result of the injection was the immediately return of her heartbeat to *normal rhythm*, while Dr. Kennedy must have felt a joyful sense of relief. The staff must have all felt elated at the results. There were no cheers or alleluias, but the smiles that filled that room told the story. They had tried everything that the ER doctors could think of, and finally at the point of giving up, *someone* thought to call her own doctor. It was only a *courtesy*. Did any of them really think he could help where they had failed?

Dr. Kennedy's first thought was this: "God used me to save Margaret. This was indeed God's doing." He realized that it wasn't anything special he had done. It had to be God looking out for Margaret. What if he had not come? If he had just accepted that the ER doctor and staff had done everything possible and not bothered to come, *Margaret would have died*. It must have been *their friendship* that had compelled him to at least come to the hospital and try to save her.

Dr. Kennedy reflected that the reason Margaret was his *favorite* patient was because of the faith in Jesus Christ that they shared. The lesson he learned from this experience was to be aware that God is working through our lives all the time. Most of the time, we are just not aware of it.

Margaret made a full recovery without any damage to her heart or after effects.

CHAPTER 27

Be Not Afraid

———— ◆ ————

Story from Tom Lukes from St. Joseph's Catholic Church in Spreckels, California, and Sacred Heart Army Chapel in Seaside, California.

For God so loved the world that he gave his only Son, so that everyone who believes in him might not perish but have eternal life. For God did not send his Son into the world to condemn the world, but that the world might be saved through him. Whoever believes in him will not be condemned; but whoever does not believe has already been condemned, because he has not believed in the name of the only Son of God.

JOHN 3:16–18

"WHO WAS THAT ON THE phone?" my wife asked. I explained that it was Sister Liliana. She had asked me to speak to the confirmation class next week. When I asked Sister what she would like me to discuss, she said she wanted me to speak on Jesus.

My first thought was that the topic was too broad. I would need to narrow the subject down to some aspect of his life, like his message or his miracles. I was not sure what would reach these young people, who were high school freshman and sophomores.

I searched my memory for a topic about Jesus that would hold the interest of the young people in the class and be something they had not already heard before. I remembered an article I had read in the *National Geographic* on the Shroud of Turin.

Some years earlier, we had taken the boys fishing to Kit Carson lodge, which was on Silver Lake near Tahoe. On the living room table of the cabin, I discovered a mixture of magazines, including a *National Geographic*. Inside was an article on the Shroud of Turin.[1] It was a fascinating story titled "The Mystery of the Shroud," by Kenneth F. Weaver.

I remember thinking that God had placed it there for me to see, because I had never even heard of the Shroud of Turin— and what a strange place to discover it. When I got home, I called the magazine and ordered three copies, one for myself and some to share with friends.

What better way to tell these young people about Jesus than to share what he suffered for us in the scourging and crucifixion? And I wouldn't just tell them about it, but I'd show them the image of the crucified figure that is visible in the shroud. I would also be able to discuss the amazing story of how the image was tested—and all the other aspects of the *National Geographic* story.

I went to Corpus Christi, the local Catholic bookstore, and found an entire book on the shroud. I had only the weekend to prepare because the following Tuesday, I was to make my presentation. I sat down and reread the June 1980 *National Geographic* article over again, and then I read the book on the shroud. I spent the following day making notes for my talk. By Sunday night I had an outline of the key elements of my talk, which I would use rather than write out the entire talk and bore the kids by reading it to them. I just hoped that I could do the subject justice.

On Monday, I was busy back at work. Before I knew it, I was standing ready to get into the shower on Tuesday morning. Just before I pulled back the curtains to get in the shower, it dawned on me that tonight after dinner I was to present my talk on Jesus. My stomach did a flip as I got in the shower. You need to understand that speaking in public was not something I did. There was something about the prospect of speaking to more than two people that really frightened me.

I often sing "Chariots of Fire" or "Amazing Grace" in the shower to start off each day, but this morning I was so nervous at the thought of having to give this talk that singing was the last thing on my mind. I said to myself, "Wait just a minute. This is crazy. My talk is on Jesus. Why not turn to Him now for help?" So I said a short prayer asking for God's blessing on my talk.

I immediately broke into song: "Be not afraid. I go before you always. Come follow me, and I will give you *peace*." What was so strange to me in that instant was that I had not thought about singing, nor had I thought about what I was to sing. Although I knew this song, I had never sung it in the shower.

I felt like God was speaking to me, saying, "Be not afraid." Also, I felt like God changed the last word of the song as I sang it. The word was *rest*, not *peace*. I was actually conscious that this was the word I was to sing, even though I knew it was the incorrect word. Once I said, "peace," I stopped singing the rest of the song. I felt strangely at peace myself, and yet minutes before I had been so nervous.

As if that were not enough to convince me that God had spoken to me through the words of the song, when I arrived at the classroom for the confirmation class later that evening, I noticed something even more shocking. The words of the song "Be Not Afraid" were written on the blackboard in the back of the space in which my talk was to be given.

---

[1] The Shroud of Turin is the purported *burial cloth of Jesus*. The image on the cloth is a *negative image* of a bearded, crucified man; so when you look at a photographic negative, you are really looking at *the positive* image, which is much more discernable. No one can explain how the image was created, but they do know that *it was not done* by any type of paint. It appears that the image was somehow *seared* onto the cloth. Some suggest that the energy of

the resurrection emanating from the body of Jesus is the only explanation.

The cloth is stained with human blood, and the image of the back and the front of a crucified man shows nail holes in the wrists and feet as well as lash marks on his back and front. The figure appears to have a broken nose as well as blood on its head right where the crown of thorns would have been.

Carbon testing in 1988 set the date of the cloth between the years 1260 and 1390. However, it was later discovered that the sample for the carbon testing was taken from *a patch* that was added much after the cloth was first discovered to repair damage from a fire. No final conclusion has ever been reached to explain the image on the cloth or to conclusively date the cloth.

CHAPTER 28

Little Angels

———•———

Story from Faye from Madonna del Sasso Catholic Church in
Salinas, California.

*Truly you have formed my inmost being; you knit me in
my mother's womb. I give you thanks that I am fearfully,
wonderfully made; wonderful are your works.*

PSALM 139:13–14

IT WAS JUST ANOTHER DAY at their house, or so it seemed.
Nana Faye was in the living room folding clothes, while her
married daughter, Jami, was in the kitchen at the sink, when
little two-and-a-half-year-old Madi came to her mommy
sobbing. Jami immediately dried her hands, knelt down, and
asked, "What's the matter, baby?"

"Mommy, Jesus hurts," Madi said.

"It's okay, Madi; where does Jesus hurt?"

Madi sobbed and said, "His knees hurt, Mommy."

She continued to cry uncontrollably. Jami hugged her tightly as she looked at Nana Faye with a questioning look. *What was this all about?*

Faye's story actually started many years before Madi was even born. It is a story of a faithful mom and dad who walk with God in constant prayer, knowing that He is with them through the trials of raising a family and continues even after their children are adults.

Ron and Faye had four children: three boys and a girl. It was when their daughter, Jami, reached puberty that the trials began. She experienced a very painful first day or two every time she had a period, missing school at least one day a month—sometimes two. She would have to be medicated and rest in bed. As she grew older, it got worse—much worse.

In her early twenties, when Faye saw Jami fall to the floor, doubled up in pain, she knew this was not normal. Her family doctor referred her to a local gynecologist in Salinas for help. He diagnosed her with endometriosis.

The laparoscopy that he later surgically performed relieved her symptoms for a time, but the real danger with endometriosis is that it might return, and if it affected the fallopian tubes and/ or the ovaries, it could prevent Jami from being able to have children. She wanted to be able to have children, especially since she was already engaged to Matthew.

By the time Jami was in her mid-twenties, the endometriosis had returned—and with it, unbearable pain. They all knew that this meant her life was in danger, or at the very least, her chance to ever have children was at risk.

With little hope of help from Jami's doctors, Faye and Ron turned to Mary's intersession with Rosaries and Chaplets of Divine Mercy[1] each day. They felt this was all they could do under the circumstances.

Then a nurse friend of Faye's told her that she had heard of a doctor involved with Respect Life, who might be able to help Jami. His name was Dr. Thomas Hilgers.[2] This gave them some hope, but it meant that Jami would have to abandon her present doctor and travel to Omaha, Nebraska, for treatment.

Initially Jami's doctor as well as the doctor for whom Faye worked were very critical of her traveling out of state to seek a doctor. "There are plenty of qualified doctors in California. Why go to Nebraska?"

When Jami's doctor learned they were talking about Dr. Hilgers, his whole response changed. "That's who is going to do Jami's surgery? How did you ever get him to see her?" He had heard Dr. Hilgers speak at a medical conference. "Dr. Hilgers is world renowned." Faye could only smile with this confirmation. *They were on the right track.* Their prayers had been answered, but they knew Jami's journey to receiving help was far from over, so the prayers continued daily.

The next step was for Jami to write a letter to Dr. Hilgers to explain her condition and submit copies of all her medical records. Then they waited. Dr. Hilgers responded that he thought his *laser procedure* could help her, but he needed more information. They had to assemble all the paperwork and lab tests and eventually be worked into his busy surgery schedule. This took over three months and resulted in a January surgery date. They realized that the delay was okay as long as he could help her.

The day Jami and Faye arrived in Omaha, it was nine degrees outside—a little cold for two California girls. They checked in at Dr. Hilgers's office. Faye was encouraged to learn that on the floor above his office, daily Mass was celebrated. She was told, "He attends Mass every day." Faye knew that her daughter would be in good hands.

Jami faced one more test to update her condition, and then she would be on to surgery the next morning. The operation lasted seven and a half hours. Dr. Hilgers spoke to Faye after the surgery: "Jami had a very severe case of endometriosis." He explained that the growths had even extended into her lower back, which explained her severe back pains. He felt that the surgery was successful, and Jami should now experience a major improvement, because all the growths had been removed.

Dr. Hilgers also explained that it was necessary to remove part of one of her ovaries, but he still believed that Jami *might* be able to conceive. However, there was no guarantee.

At least there was a chance that Jami might still be able to have children. Faye knew that this was much better than what had been offered to them back in Salinas. Their trip to Omaha had been successful. In fact, Dr. Hilgers and the Catholic hospital even waived all charges that were not covered by Jami's insurance.

After nine days of recovery, Faye and Jami returned to Salinas on another very cold Nebraska morning. Waiting for them at the airport in San Jose were Matthew and Jami's father, Ron. They were tired and happy to be back home. Now it was time for Jami to rest and get back her strength.

Jami and Matthew were married the following October. *She felt healthy again!* The pain was gone. Several months later, they learned that Jami was pregnant. Dr. Hilgers was right! Months later Jami's miracle baby boy was born. They named him Isaiah Matthew. He weighed nearly six pounds and was the delight of the family.

On February 1, when Isaiah was four years old and Jami was thirty-three, she announced that she was pregnant for a second time. This came as a real shock, because everyone thought a second pregnancy was not even possible because of the surgery.

In the following month, it became clear that this was not going to be a normal pregnancy. Jami had started bleeding. As Faye put it, "She was bleeding a lot." They even feared that she might have lost the baby. Her doctor immediately scheduled an ultrasound at the Imaging Center in Salinas.

Faye took off work to be with Jami. For a few minutes, they *sat alone* in the imaging room and waited. *Faye prayed silently.* When the technician arrived, it was all business. Jami explained the situation. The ultrasound transducer moved across her tummy as they all watched the monitor. "I have a heartbeat...*No*, I have *two* heartbeats!" Jami had not lost her baby; she had gained one! Jami and her Mom began crying together. This was another miracle—but one that might challenge all of them in the coming months.

Jami was referred to a doctor to San Francisco who specialized in multiple births. He said the babies were healthy and about thirteen weeks along. The next day, they went to Monterey to see Dr. Keith who would become Jami's ob-gyn. He would deliver her babies when the time came. Jami's bleeding continued and with it daily Rosaries and Chaplets were being raised up. Nana Faye, the family, and close friends were constantly praying for the two little ones.

The major crisis of the pregnancy was when the doctor discovered that two of the four ventricles in the babies' brains measured slightly larger than normal. This was compounded by the fact that the two little ones were not gaining weight as they should. The doctor urged Jami to undergo an amniocentesis test to be sure the babies were normal.

When Jami asked, "If I take the test and you find that there is something wrong, is there anything you can do to help my babies?"

He replied, "No."

She felt she had to ask the question one more time, but she received the same answer. So Jami said, "Then *I will not have the test*. I want my babies just the way they are." She would never allow any harm to come to them.

The continued concern for the babies, who by now had been identified as baby girls, led Isaiah to beg Nana, "Please ask Jesus to come into the hearts of the babies." Isaiah was concerned about his little sisters. Somehow this little four-year-old knew that Jesus could help, so Nana prayed with him.

The original due date was October 4, the feast of St. Gianna Beretta Molla,³ so Matthew and Jami decided to name the first baby Gianna and the second Madi, which was short for Madeline. By late August, the doctor told Jami that the babies were not getting enough nourishment from her placentas. On August 25, Madi's heart rate was really low, and Dr. Keith said *it was time*.

Matthew was with Jami in the delivery room for the C-section.

Faye waited in the adjacent room but was not able to see anything because the blinds were drawn. At 12:45, the blinds opened to reveal two tiny baby girls.

Faye said, "I gasped with a big breath of relief and cried like a baby. I was all by myself. I was just overwhelmed with tears of joy. I was so thankful to God."

The doctor told Nana Faye that the babies were doing "really well, considering how small they are." Gianna weighed three pounds, six ounces, while Madi weighed three pounds. God had helped them face one crisis after another during Jami's pregnancy, resulting in two tiny little angels.

---

[1] Chaplet of Divine Mercy is a Catholic devotion to the Divine Mercy of Jesus, based on the apparitions of Jesus reported by Saint Faustina Kowalska (1905–1938), known as "the Apostle of Mercy." For the actual prayer that is to be said using a Rosary go to: www.thedivinemercy.org.

[2] Thomas W. Hilgers, MD, is the founder and director of the Pope Paul VI Institute for the Study of Human Reproduction, where he is also the senior medical consultant in obstetrics, gynecology, and reproductive medicine and surgery.

Since the time of his first research in the natural regulation of human fertility in 1968 as a senior medical student, he co-developed the Creighton Model FertilityCare™ System (Source: Wikipedia).

³ St. Gianna Beretta Molla (1922–1962) was an Italian pediatrician. When she was pregnant with her fourth child, Molla refused both an abortion and a hysterectomy, despite knowing that continuing with the pregnancy could result in her own death, as it in fact did.

The miracle recognized by the Catholic Church to canonize Gianna Molla involved a mother, Elizabeth Comparini, who was sixteen weeks pregnant in 2003. She sustained a tear in her placenta that drained her womb of all amniotic fluid. Because a normal term of pregnancy is forty weeks, Comparini was told by her doctors that the baby's chance of survival was nil. Comparini said she prayed to Gianna Molla, asking for her intercession, and she was able to deliver a healthy baby despite the lack of amniotic fluid. Gianna Molla was canonized as a saint of the Roman Catholic Church in 2004 (Source: Wikipedia).

CHAPTER 29

Prayers and Rainbows

Story from Will Souza from St. Joseph's Catholic Church in
Spreckels, California

> *Rejoice always, pray without ceasing. In all circumstances give*
> *thanks, for this is the will of God for you in Christ Jesus.*

1 THESSALONIANS 5:16–18

SALINAS IS KNOWN FOR JOHN Steinbeck, who wrote about
the Salinas Valley in many of his books, such as *East of Eden*
and *The Grapes of Wrath*, but today, the Salinas Valley is also
famous as the salad capital of the world.

The soil in the Salinas Valley is dark and rich. Much of the lettuce consumed by the United States is raised here. The valley
extends ninety miles from the ocean in the north to King City
in the south. The prime lettuce is grown in the area surrounding Salinas, which includes the little town of Spreckels.

Spreckels is located just three miles from Salinas. It has a population of nearly seven hundred. It is where Will Souza lives, works, and attends church at St. Joseph's Catholic Church with his wife, Diane.

This church, although in a small town, serves a population well beyond the boundaries of the town. The view from the front door of the church looks out on acres of fields of lettuce that extend to the old Spreckels sugar plant silos beyond. The Spreckels plant shut down in 1982 after producing sugar from sugar beets for more than a hundred years.

Will was a research assistant in the seed lab of a major produce company in Spreckels for over ten years. With red, green, romaine, and head lettuce being the staple crops in the valley, it is no surprise that seed research and development were an important part of the salad industry.

On this particular day, Will was not thinking about *lettuce*. He was thinking about *his job*. A recent slowdown made all those at the Spreckels company fear for their jobs. The most recently hired are usually the first fired but not always, so when rumors circulate in the office, everyone fears for his or her job.

The rumors of layoffs had started some months earlier. Will had lived with this before, but the subtle stress was real, and it affected him, even though he tried not to let it. So on Friday, when he was called in to his supervisor's office, he was not surprised to be laid off with four other employees.

It didn't help much that he had anticipated this move. It still hurt. On the bright side, he still had his vacation days and two weeks of severance pay to help for a while. Now the only question in Will's mind was whether he could find another job before those days with pay ran out.

Once Diane heard the news of his layoff, she immediately got on the phone and called all their friends to ask for prayer for Will's job search. That night Will too went to God in prayer. "God said that I would be employed in a short time, and I would really love what I would be doing." This answer gave Will a real sense of peace that overcame his fears and concerns.

The next day, Will decided to get started with the job search. He decided to start his job search at a large produce company in Salinas where he already knew some of the staff because his former company worked with them on a regular basis.

Upon entering the lobby, Will explained that he was there because he was seeking employment in the research department. A call was made, and soon a woman came into the lobby. She handed Will an application to fill in and then left Will to allow him time to complete it; but before he was even finished, she reappeared and asked Will to come with her to meet with her supervisor, who wanted to meet with Will.

Will's interview had just begun when the supervisor was interrupted by a phone call from Will's old boss, who was apparently unaware that Will was there. He wanted to let the supervisor know that he had been forced to lay off some staff members, but the Spreckles company was still solvent. The call was perfectly timed for Will, because it confirmed to the supervisor that he was laid off because of *the slowdown*, not because he was *incompetent* or was a problem.

When Will came home after the interview, he told Diane that he thought it had gone well, especially because of the chance phone call from his old boss. Later in the day, Will received a phone call from the new company. They asked him to return Monday for a second interview.

As it turned out, the second interview was actually a salary and benefits negotiation. Will was hired and asked to start on the following day. So on Tuesday, he headed in to work, only to notice a rainbow right over his new place of employment. "That is a nice sign," he thought.

Later in the morning, Will was accompanied on a trip out of the office to another part of Salinas by a coworker who wanted to show Will the location of a company that Will would be visiting as part of his new job. On their return, he noticed that there was another rainbow directly over his new workplace.

Considering how rarely Will ever saw rainbows in Salinas, two rainbows in one day were more than coincidence. Will saw this as a confirmation that this job was what God had wanted for him. He looked forward to the time in the new job.

CHAPTER 30

Baptism of Fire

———◦•◦———

Story from Michael Hagerty, Music Director at Sacred Heart
Army Chapel in Seaside, California.

> *And they were all filled with the holy Spirit and began to speak*
> *in different tongues, as the Spirit enabled them to proclaim.*
> *They were astounded, and in amazement they asked, "Are*
> *not all of these people who are speaking Galileans? Then how*
> *does each of us hear them in his own native language?"*

ACTS 2:4, 7

St. Augustine's Catholic Church in Pleasanton,
California, was overflowing with some 1,300 to 1,400
people, even though the church was only intended to seat
nine hundred. All the side aisles were full, and the back of
the church was three to four people deep. This had become a
regular Sunday occurrence. Now Communion was being distributed, and the spirit of God was again tangibly present. The
music seemed to call God's children forward for communion:

"Come to the Water"

You said you'd come and share all my sorrows
You said you'd be there for all my tomorrows
I came so close to sending you away
But just like you promised, you came here to stay
I just had to pray

And Jesus said, "Come to the water, stand by my side
I know you are thirst, you won't be denied
I felt every tear drop, when in darkness you cried
and I strove to remind you,
It's for those tears I died."

MARSHA J. STEVENS

Michael was playing lead guitar and singing as part of the parish's own music group. It was clear to Michael that something had happened in his parish church that had transformed it in the past year or year and a half, but more importantly, he knew that he had changed too. This is his story.

Michael was one of six kids in the family, with his sister being the youngest, while he was the second oldest of five boys. They lived across from St. Augustine's Church, so it was not surprising then that all five boys were altar servers. The family's close proximity to the church and the boys' service to their pastor provided a natural reason for the pastor to drop over for dinner with the Hagertys.

In the 1960s, it was quite common for Catholics to have large families. Perhaps this was partially the reason that parents encouraged their children to enter religious life. There would always be plenty of grandchildren, even if one of their boys became a priest. At twelve years old, Michael was more interested in learning to play the guitar than thinking seriously about any calling to the priesthood. "Music was huge in my life." This was also a time when *American Bandstand* and rock stars were very much a part of the youth scene.

Even so, when Michael was thirteen or fourteen, "I sensed a calling in my life." So he entered the high school seminary boarding school, where he lived away from home. This had been brought about in part by his pastor, who always encouraged him to consider the priesthood. Those home visits to the Hagertys had finally paid off, in the mind of his pastor.

While in the seminary, Michael did not abandon his guitar skills. The seminary actually facilitated his skills, especially because of the advent of the folk Mass, which was new to the Catholic Church—a direct result of Vatican II changes. He became part of the group that played at the folk Mass. It was here that he refined his music skills. Michael remembers that "My upper classmates in high school were really good guitar players."

After two years in the seminary, Michael returned home. He missed his family and friends. "I just decided that I didn't want to go in that direction." He finished his last two years of high school in public school, while continuing to work on his musical talents.

Michael was glad that he was raised Catholic because it created a sound foundation for his life. Upon reflecting on those early years of his life, it was clear that the way he lived as a Catholic was not always for the right motives. He felt that he was raised on the concept of *doing our duty* rather than out of *love of God*. This attitude was probably an outgrowth of wanting to follow the Commandments and his genuine concern for the focus on *sin in his life*.

Michael knew that he was not alone in this struggle. He was aware that many adults seemed to have a similar attitude. You could push the Church rules to a point, but as long as you went to church on Sunday, you were all right. He became a little discouraged by this realization of his attitude.

As Michael moved into his later high school years, he too found himself pushing the limits of the Church's laws. Beer parties and carousing became a regular part of his life. Michael described himself during this time as *of the world*. But since he still lived at home, he felt obligated to attend church. It was all part of the house rules: "If you live at home, you *will* go to church."

It was about this time that Michael was invited to join a musical group that played at Sunday Mass at St. Augustine's. There were five in the group. Michael played lead guitar and sang.

One of Michael's brothers played drums. There was also a second guitar player and a bass guitarist. Jim was lead vocalist.

They played mainly *Christian music* with some secular music mixed in. They called themselves "The Second Collection." The band's name was chosen because it was something that most Catholics could relate to. They were so popular that they even recorded two albums of their church music.

Jim was the oldest member of the band in his mid-to-late thirties. He acted not only as the lead vocalist but as the band director. In his regular life, he was a very successful marketing executive. He was married with five kids, but he had a very rocky family life because Jim was an alcoholic.

In desperation, his wife talked Jim into attending a Marriage Encounter, which was not intended to deal with alcoholism or even a rocky marriage but was intended to help restore the love that might have faded over the years.

When Jim came back from the weekend, he and his wife discovered that they had fallen deeply in love again. "God used Marriage Encounter (ME) to open their hearts to Him, more of God, more of love, forgiving, and all of those things that He brings." But that was not all that God had in store for Jim. Next, ME friends invited Jim and his wife to a *Catholic Charismatic Renewal*[1] prayer meeting. When they asked what that was, the response was "Just consider it the next step."

It was there that Jim received *the baptism of the Holy Spirit*.[2] He began speaking in tongues, he was instantly delivered from his alcoholism, his marriage was healed even more, and "he was filled with the power of God and hunger for his Word."

When Jim returned to the music group the next weekend, it was clear that he had changed drastically. He seemed to glow with joy. As Michael put it, "He was on fire for God, but none of them wanted anything to do with him."

They all were content with how things had been going. They felt like they were doing plenty already. "We go to church, we're serving God, and the people love our music and are being blessed." In other words, Michael and the music group *did not want to change*. Perhaps Jim's transformation scared them at the time. Michael said they could see that Jim was changed, but as long as that didn't affect the group, they were fine with it.

As leader of the group, Jim immediately made changes in the music that they played and sang—no more secular music, only *Jesus songs*. The group was fine with that, since the secular music had been very limited anyway. Michael explained that one priest wrote about the secular influence that came about because of the misinterpretation of Vatican II: "The Church made a mistake. They tried to bring the *world* into the Church to try to change it, instead of the reverse—bringing *the Church* into the world to change it." So Jim was on the right path, and he was leading the group beginning in this small way, but more leading and experiences were still to come.

The story of Jim's charismatic encounter and healing from alcoholism was soon known by others in the Charismatic Movement—"In the early to mid-1970s, the Holy Spirit was being poured out on every denomination [not just Catholics]." In fact, the Catholics were late to receive this outpouring, compared to some of the Protestants.

Jim was asked to come and share his testimony at other prayer meetings and other charismatic events. Once word got out that Jim was the leader of a musical group that played *Jesus music*, he was encouraged to bring the group to their charismatic prayer meetings.[3]

When Jim approached Michael and the other group members to see if they would be willing to play at a charismatic prayer group (for free), they all agreed, although none of them really knew what he was getting into. The first prayer meeting brought the group to an event where everyone acted like Jim had. As Michael shared, "It was weird—they were smiling and saying, 'Praise the Lord,' or 'Yes, Jesus!' or 'Jesus, Jesus, Jesus.' They were all filled with the joy of Jesus." During the prayer meeting, people were singing in tongues or praying in tongues while they lifted their hands up to God.

Needless to say, Michael and the group were *very* uncomfortable with this. Michael and the group thought, "What has Jim got us into?" But even though the band felt this was all very strange, they continued to come with Jim to the prayer meetings. Perhaps it was because the people loved the music. "The

Lord anointed it powerfully! While we were at these meetings, the people experienced the presence of God that filled that space." Michael admitted, "I didn't recognize it, but I knew something special was happening." Michael explained, "It was so foreign, and we were uncomfortable around it. Plus most of us were pretty young." When they weren't playing music, all the band members but Jim would go outside, hang out, and just get away from what was going on inside.

For about a year and a half, the group played at these events. In fact, "We were instantly thrust into a regional and statewide evangelistic music ministry!" As time went by, Michael actually looked forward to being part of the experience. The event that finally piqued Michael's interest occurred when he heard a woman speak of the *end times.*

Jim told Michael to read Joel 3:1, which reads, "Then afterward I will pour out my spirit upon all mankind. Your sons and daughters shall prophesy, your old men shall dream dreams, your young men shall see visions. Even upon the servants and the handmaids, in those days, I will pour out my spirit." In Michael's mind this verse not only pointed to what he had seen and heard at these prayer meetings, but it raised issues of *end times,* which frightened him. Jim offered to help explain *end times* to all of them.

Jim spent three evenings in a row sharing his insights with the music group, and eventually Jim gave Michael a book to read on the subject. The night after playing at a day-long prayer meeting, Michael sat down to read the book. Immediately, he said, "I had this headache that just showed up, and then all of a sudden my eyes were crossing." It seemed that the devil really didn't want Michael to read this book!

He remembered the scripture quote, "If you ask anything in my name, I will do it." (Jn 14:14). So Michael prayed, "Can you take away my headache, so I can read this book? In an instant, I sensed this churning right where the pain was near my forehead and temple area. Then it slowly entered and displaced the pain with what others describe as 'liquid love.' That's exactly what it felt like! It was warm, and I just started shaking, and tears started coming down." Overcome with emotion over the experience, Michael completely forgot about any desire to read the book, but instead he thanked Jesus and prayed, "I invite you into my heart, and I sensed that same Holy Spirit enter my being, and it brought my heart to peace."

Time stood still as Michael was overwhelmed by God's love in this warm feeling of peace. Eventually, it subsided. Michael called Jim to share with him his experience. Jim confirmed that Michael had received *the baptism of the Holy Spirit*, which he himself had received more than a year earlier.

Jim had said that the gift of tongues didn't always manifest right away but Michael should ask God for tongues and be open to receive it or any of the other "gifts of the Holy Spirit"[4]. So, that evening at home, Michael tried to make sounds that were similar to what he had heard others speak. Nothing worked! Frustrated he spoke to God, "Lord I give up...It must not be for me, so I am not even going to try [again]." He didn't even finish the sentence, when the first syllable "...popped out of my mouth. Tongues started coming out. I sensed the same spirit of God as I prayed in this new language."

Michael was only twenty-two at the time. Now, more than thirty years later, Michael speaks enthusiastically about what God has done and continues to do in his life. He plays worship music every Sunday at Sacred Heart Army Chapel at the 11:00 a.m. Mass and leads the music at a prayer meeting every Tuesday night in Alamo. The experience of the baptism in the Holy Spirit changed his life forever and clearly still affects him today.

Michael's final thoughts: Everyone *who is in Christ* has the capacity to move in all the Gifts. The Spirit distributes the manifestation at different times according to the need. *Tongues* has multiple uses (public, private, etc.) It is the only charismatic gift that also builds up the believer himself (as a prayer language). I still hold to the truth that, anyone who desires the gift of tongues can receive it. It only takes an environment that welcomes it, and a yielding and abandonment to the Holy Spirit.

[1] The "Catholic Charismatic Renewal" began at a retreat in 1967, when two Duquesne University professors participated in a retreat where they called

on God to send the Holy Spirit on them. This outpouring of the Holy Spirit was similar to what happened to the apostles at Pentecost, as described in chapter 2 of Acts. It rapidly spread to other Catholics at Duquesne and then to Notre Dame University. By the early 1970s, it had spread throughout the United States.

The book *God Loves You and There's Nothing You Can Do about It*, by David Mangan, deals with the personal experience of one of the Duquesne professors. A second book, on the baptism of the Holy Spirit and its effect on a person's life, is the inspiring autobiography of Fr. Michael Scanlon, entitled *Let the Fire Fall*.

The Vatican accepted the Charismatic Movement in 1998. In May 2004, during vespers on the eve of Pentecost, Pope Saint John Paul II said, "Thanks to the Charismatic Movement, a multitude of Christians, men and women, young people and adults, have rediscovered Pentecost as a living reality in their daily lives. I hope that the spirituality of Pentecost will spread in the Church as a renewed incentive to prayer, holiness, communion, and proclamation" (Homily of John Paul II, Celebration of First Vespers of Pentecost, Saturday, May 29, 2004, no.3, www.vatican.va.).

[2] "Baptism of the Holy Spirit" refers to the fulfillment of the sacraments of baptism and confirmation, when the Holy Spirit is released by God in all its fullness, similar to what happened at Pentecost and as promised by Jesus when he said, in Acts 1:8, "But you will receive power when the Holy Spirit has come upon you; and you shall be my witnesses...to the ends of the earth." It is this event, where God manifests himself powerfully, that an individual experiences the "baptism of the Holy Spirit." It normally occurs with the laying on of hands, but it can also happen as a result of personal prayer asking for the release of the Holy Spirit.

[3] "Charismatic prayer meeting" refers to a gathering of individuals who either have received the "baptism of the Holy Spirit" or who seek to participate in prayer and praise God. Such a meeting consists of using the gifts of the Holy Spirit, songs of praise, and worship.

[4] "Gifts of the Holy Spirit" refers to the gifts that are referenced in the 1Cor 12:8-11, "To one the Spirit gives wisdom in discourse, to another the power to express knowledge. Through the Spirit one receives faith; by the same Spirit another is given the gift of healing, and still another, miraculous powers. Prophecy is given to one; to another power to distinguish one spirit from another. One receives the gift of tongues, another that of interpreting the tongues. But it is the one and same Spirit who produces all these gifts, distributing them to each as he wills."

CHAPTER 31

Dedication to Our Lady

Story from Tom Lukes from St. Joseph's Catholic Church in Spreckels, California, and Sacred Heart Army Chapel in Seaside, California.

Prayer to the Holy Spirit[1]

*Come Holy Spirit enlighten my heart, to
see the things, which are of God.
Come Holy Spirit into my mind that I may
know the things that are of God.
Come Holy Spirit into my soul that I belong only to God.
Sanctify all that I think, say, and do that all
will be for the glory of God. Amen.*

About three weeks ago, I began getting up at 5:30 a.m. to set aside half an hour to pray before going to work. The first morning, I noticed that the birds start to sing at exactly 5:30. I soon began to associate my early rise to be simply joining with the birds to say my *good morning* to God. The only difference was that they sang, while I prayed and read. We were *both* praising our Creator, our Lord and God.

Their early-morning singing made it easier to get up so early. In fact, I began to hear the birds before the alarm would even go off, so I began to get up without disturbing my wife. I am sure God was simply using his creatures to help me get an early start. I knew in my heart that I needed this time with God to start my day off on the right foot.

About a week into my new early-morning prayer time, I received *at work* a 2003 catalog from Queenship Publishing. The catalog is a great collection of Catholic publications that include books, audiotapes, and videos for sale. When I noticed that I wasn't getting to look it at work, I decided to bring it home and put it with my reading material for my prayer time. The next morning, I soon found myself looking through the catalog for at least ten minutes, when on page 19, I came across a small picture of a booklet called *In the End My Immaculate Heart Will Triumph*, followed by a description of the book.

I said to myself, "I have seen this booklet before." I paused and looked on the coffee table in front of me, and there was the very booklet. I knew it had looked familiar, but I had no idea how or when it got there. To this day, I cannot tell you how it got there or who gave it to me. Of course, I reached over to see what the little book was about.

It turned out to be a thirty-three-day preparation for the dedication of the reader to the Immaculate Heart of Mary. There was a different reading for each day, followed by some of the most beautiful prayers I had ever read. I decided that it looked interesting. I thought that I might start reading it in the morning on the following day, April 28th.

So the next morning, I skimmed through the first few pages and discovered a schedule that was entitled "Daily Calendar: Six Suggested Schedules for Consecration." As it turned out, the first day of the preparation (day one) needed to be on a specific date, because the dedication was scheduled to end on day thirty-four, which was always a Marian feast day. I almost jumped out of my chair when I noticed that the fourth suggested schedule started on April 28, which was that very day. *What a coincidence!*

I knew God must really want me to dedicate myself to the Immaculate Heart of Our Lady, so I got started. When I got to the prayer to the Holy Spirit (see opening prayer), I was amazed at the beauty and simplicity of the prayer. I simply melted with its power and truth. It was the most beautiful prayer that I had ever read. When I finished day one, I shared the coincidence with my wife, Lois.

I began to realize what the chances were of what had just happened:

❧ There are only six days in the entire 365 days of the year that this could happen.

❧ I don't even know where the devotional booklet came from—and neither did Lois. I don't remember ordering it.

❧ The Queenship catalog also just happened to arrive at the right time. Wow!

Since this experience, I have gone through the dedication on four occasions, and each time, I know the time spent draws me closer to Jesus through Our Lady.

God knows what we need in our lives, and sometimes, to get our attention, He lets us know in a profound way.

————•————

[1] This prayer was given by Our Lady to the visionaries at Medjugorje on December 23, 1991 (From the booklet titled *In the End My Immaculate Heart Will Triumph.*)

ACKNOWLEDGMENTS

———•———

I AM ESPECIALLY GRATEFUL TO MY wife, Lois, who spent hours doing the initial proofing of this document and being a loving critic. I am extremely indebted to Gloria Boyer for the final editing and her many helpful comments.

Thanks also to my attorney brother, Bob, for advising me in all the copyright and other legal issues that relate to using other people's stories in my book, and Travis J. Vanden Heuvel with Peregrino Press, my publisher, for recognizing the value of the stories in God Incidents and being willing to publish it.

I want to thank Fr. Mike Miller for being willing in his busy schedule as pastor to not only share his story ("The Hitchhiker") with me but to offer council in aspects of this book. I also want to thank all the friends and my sister, Terry, who encouraged me with their words and comments.

I want to thank the Most Reverend Richard J. Garcia, D.D., Bishop of the Diocese of Monterey, for writing the introduction to this book and spending time with me discussing the book.

Finally, I especially need to thank all the *storytellers* who were willing to share their "God incidents" with me. Without the *storytellers*, this book would not have been possible.

EPILOGUE

A s I READ THROUGH THE stories again during the *final editing*, I had the desire not to stop here, but to consider other stories from my brothers and sisters, who would want to share his/her story in a second book.

If you are interested in commenting on, *or* you would like to share your *own story* with me for *God Incidents 2 – More True Stories of God Working in the Lives of Catholics*, drop me an email at ShareGodIncidents@gmail.com with your comments, or just tell me a very brief recap of your own "God Incident".

In any event, I hope you enjoyed reading about what God has done in the lives of us, His children. I look forward to hearing from you. Otherwise, start looking for God *incidents* in your own life.

Thomas R. Lukes

ABOUT THE AUTHOR

THOMAS R. LUKES IS A lifelong Catholic and a retired architect. He worked on many church related and school projects. When he was thirty, he had a special encounter with God that motivated him to live his life for God while serving his church. Today, he serves as lector and Eucharistic minister at his parish.

For five years, he served as "lay director" of the Cursillo movement in Monterey, California, and was editor of the Cursillo newsletter, which he named *Rekindle*. In 2011, Lukes was part of Bishop Richard Garcia's committee to bring Immaculate Heart Radio to the Monterey bay area. Proceeds from this book go to support Catholic education for the diocese.

Lukes and his wife have three sons and six grandchildren. In his retirement, Lukes enjoys daily Mass, weekly Bible studies, reading, and, of course, golf.

CPSIA information can be obtained
at www.ICGtesting.com
Printed in the USA
LVOW13*2131170518
577561LV00009B/259/P

DEAR
Lessons
from
Your Child's
Teacher
PARENTS...

THE PARENT AND TEACHER GUIDE
TO CREATING A BETTER BOND

CHRISTINA SINGH, Ed.D

ISBN: 978-1-7361714-0-0

Singh. Christina.
Dear Parents ... Lessons from Your Child's Teacher

Edited by: Melissa Long

Published by Warren Publishing
Charlotte, NC
www.warrenpublishing.net
Printed in the United States

This book is dedicated, first and foremost, to the committed parents and teachers (and teacher-parents of course) who wake up early and stay up late every day for their children. Where would teachers be without parents? Where would parents be without teachers? It's a team effort. Thank you!

ACKNOWLEDGMENTS

I would like to express my sincere gratitude to my co-teachers who have treated me and my students with kindness and respect throughout the years. It is not always easy to modify assignments, alter schedules, and provide individual support often on a moment's notice, but you do it. You do it with grace and respect. Without question, I have been one of the lucky ones to have a positive relationship with countless classroom and special education teachers. You are the ones I lean on for support. You are the ones—the active parents—who have made my teaching journey so rewarding. You are the ones who work together with me for our shared children. You are the ones who ask for help and work diligently to help your children grow. Your efforts allow your children to develop into the best versions of themselves.

I would like to acknowledge that this book is also for the students. For those of you who have a supportive and loving environment where you can ask for help with homework, you are the lucky ones. For those students who are lost—alone on an island—you have the power and control. Keep pushing forward in school. Get that degree and go for the career your heart desires. Grow up, become successful, and build your own families with the people you choose and who choose you. You can do it and you deserve it. You don't know what the future holds, but know that it will get better.

Thank you to the professionals who made this book possible, the people who allowed me to spread my message of hope and cooperation. Mindy, Melissa, Amy, and everyone else who touched my book in any way—I am grateful. You saw this book as I did: a way to begin rebuilding the relationship between parents and teachers.

Finally, but possibly the most important, I would like to thank my family: Daryl, Angel, and Sara. For the better part of two decades you have provided me with the support and confidence to pursue my dreams. We have traveled across continents and I could not imagine this world without any one of you. To Cammy, though you came into my world much later, your impact has not been less. To my sisters Kathy and Dawn, who have stood by my side since the day I was born, you are my confidants and fiercest champions; my existence would not be complete without you both. To my former dissertation chairman, Dr. Robert Krell, you believed in me from start to finish. Thank you. To the friends I call family: the military life can be a lonely one, but you never let that happen. You know who you are—Garner, Guzman, Latter, Morrissette-Utter, Newman, Polk, Rivera, Villanueva, Tucker, Wolf-Faircloth—thank you.

PROLOGUE

I chose to write about this topic due to the recent parent and teacher interactions I have both witnessed and been told about. Teachers and parents seem to be on different pages of the book; some are in completely different books! However, I believe if each knew how the other side felt, it might be the first step in bridging the gap and finally getting down to the most important thing for both sides—the child. Parents need teachers, and teachers need parents.

Teaching is a wonderful profession, one that is rewarding and memorable. It's also one that is not always respected by society. Long gone are the days when students were in trouble for failing grades. It is more common today to see teachers and schools on the hook if the students are failing any given subject. I am hoping this will change. This country needs great teachers who stay in the profession and retire happy and fulfilled with a lifetime of successful students to look back on. Students deserve to learn from veteran teachers.

If both parents and teachers take anything away from this book, please take this: It's about building relationships and it takes two—or three if there are two parents. It is never too late to pick up the pieces of this relationship. It is too important.

If you are a parent, grandparent, or guardian, if you have students enrolled in public, charter, or private school, this pertains to you.

While reading this, I ask two things of you. Whether you are a teacher or a parent or perhaps both, please keep an open mind and be honest with yourself. This book is not meant to be critical of anyone. It is about fixing a broken system of many broken, stressed-out people. It is about starting with the bottom and working up for the mutual benefit of all included. It is about creating awareness of something you might not even realize is going on around you.

CHAPTER 1

Teachers Love Their Students

Truth, teachers (mostly) love their profession and the little people they (hopefully) inspire every day. I'll get to the small percentage who don't love the job and students in a later chapter. Yes, they do exist, but for this chapter, it's safe to assume these teachers are one of the vast majority who did not consciously choose this high-paying profession for the wrong reasons.

Here's a riddle: What do teachers and parents have in common?

Do you give up? They both are involved in the growth and development of a particular child.

Think back to the last time you sat through a parent-teacher conference or attended a school event.

Was your child's teacher present after school hours and smiling? Was your child's teacher attentive to the needs of your child and dedicated to their well-being? I hope that as you are reading this, images are coming to mind that are positive and helpful in your own confusing journey as a parent. If they are not, there are strategies I will provide that may aid in the rebuilding of this negative relationship. Don't give up on me now—we are only on the second page.

In order to become a teacher, an individual must attend a four-year college or university and complete a student teaching internship. This is the bare minimum. The internship equates to free labor in the classroom that provides real-world experience with a seasoned professional. It also serves as an eye-opener before you start teaching as to hours, work expectations, lesson plans and prep time, and teacher-student interaction. After all, there is no substitute for on-the-job training. Since they put themselves through all of this, why would someone who doesn't want to teach continue forward? Some would surmise it's because they want long summer vacations or holidays off. If that's the case, buckle up! It's going to be a long thirty years.

While teachers do enjoy taking a vacation and detoxing from life in general, I can speak from personal experience: that is not the primary focus of daily life in school as a teacher. Of course, what person does not enjoy a few days escaping work, stress, and maybe even family? Maybe you? What are your thoughts?

This statement—taking a few days off to escape—can apply to for just about any profession. The best teachers do not spend the better part of three months sitting on a beach with a cocktail. In fact, most spend their free time, including the summer, working to perfect their craft or working a summer job to make ends meet. Much of a teacher's mental and emotional energy is often spent on their students and not on their cocktail. Some of the mental and emotional energy is reserved for financial issues, so don't worry—your child is not the only thing keeping teachers awake at night. The concern is that some school districts only provide the option of a ten-month salary. That means two months out of the year, no income coming in. The problem is not the teachers; the problem is not the students; and the problem is not the parents.

The problem is that everyone is living on their own island without access to the others' perspectives. This is where I come in. I've been a parent, and I've been a teacher. In today's society, both parenting and the education system are under attack. Every day, the news and social media of all kinds is filled with negative stories of teachers, bus drivers, or schools and, sometimes, all of the above in one news segment. Some have to do with the amount of testing, money spent, or the unfortunate inappropriate acts of staff members who did not act like the professionals they were supposed to be. I am not saying these people never behaved this way. However, such horrendous acts do not occur in every school and classroom.

Think about it this way. When you were younger, would you have liked to be blamed for a sibling's wrongdoing? I would imagine not. That is exactly what is occurring here. One parent or teacher expresses poor judgment, and everyone is to blame. That hardly seems reasonable.

There is also constant argument and the passing along of misinformation as to what constitutes a public, charter, or private school. Parents and staff members bash each other just like mothers in the "mommy wars." Does it matter who works and who is a stay-at-home mom? The same concept applies here. Do what you want and put your child where you think they fit best. If another parent has a differing opinion, well, that is for them to choose and not for you to judge. For example, I am constantly asked if private schools or charter schools allow students with disabilities into their classrooms as pupils. Much of what people talk about has no foundational basis in truth or fact. Rather, it is the opinionated word of mouth that spreads, just like gossip. We all know how that goes.

The same can be said for parents. What I cannot stress enough is that all teachers, or all parents, should not be held accountable for the mistakes of one or even a small percentage of them. The actions of one are just that, the actions of one. That one individual should not hold hostage the reputation of an entire profession in the judgment of the public eye. I caution you to please consider this. Once again, would you want to be judged unfairly because a friend or family member did an unspeakable act? I would hope not. I have seen countless articles shaming parents for allowing devices at the dinner table in a restaurant or "mishandling" a temper tantrum in public. It seems that no one really wants to hear the other side; rather, the loudest person wins out.

In the end, the biggest losers are the students, and that is the real tragedy here. This is what both sides need to understand. Teachers, you spend at least six hours a day with other people's children—the most treasured reason for living and the most important people in their parents' lives. That concept must be taken seriously, and the fact that you will take good care of them needs to be conveyed to the parents. Now parents, this does not mean your children are perfect or you can verbally abuse your child's teacher because you did not get your way. The teacher is not the enemy, nor is the teacher attacking your child when they have something to say that may not be positive. Next time you are sitting across the table or desk from your child's teacher and you hear about how your child has been chatting during class lessons, remember that the teacher is saying this to help your child learn skills, such as self-control, patience, and listening. In a few years, what do you think will happen if your child continues with this behavior and speaks out of turn while in a meeting with their boss? Well, your child will end up back at home, unemployed and living in your basement, and that's the truth. Now, instead of the boss, what if it's the client? Would you hire someone to sell or renovate your home if they did not listen to you but, instead, constantly spoke over you? I can honestly say that would be a "no" for me. News flash: while schools do allow appropriate times for socializing, during a teacher's lesson is not one of them. Your child likely already knows this. Learning how to listen and communicate is not a school lesson but a life lesson.

RAISE YOUR HAND IF YOU ARE PERFECT.

Parents, where do you see your child in the next five, ten, or even thirty years? Can you imagine a confident, articulate individual sitting in a college class? Can you see your child as the boss of a company? How do you think your child is going to behave in these places? By disrespecting adults at school? By hurting or mistreating their peers? Nope, that is absolutely not the way to do it. That type of behavior will have them living under your roof either unemployed or underemployed. Either way, you are footing the bill for their food, clothing, and anything else they will want or need, such as medical care. More than likely, there is no medical, dental, vision, or 401K in the profession of professional couch potato. What if you see your child as a doctor or a lawyer? Do you think not completing homework or classwork will prepare them for this level of education? Perhaps not, and I use that phrase lovingly. Even before they enter kindergarten, students learn how to intellectually, socially, and behaviorally navigate the classroom.

Students need boundaries. These boundaries provide structure and security. Children test these boundaries, and if there is no boundary, they will view you and everyone in their wake as pushovers. Please consider how to help your children develop into kind, caring, and independent adults who will love you and care for you as you enter your golden years.

Here are some tips that I hope you would consider.

Please remember that if you are not already doing these things and would like to begin, introduce them slowly and give your child a chance to adapt. If you are already doing them, then you deserve a high five, handshake, slap on the back, or any other way you would want to be congratulated. You are raising an independent child who should be able to take care of you and change those old-people diapers when you need them.

TIP #1: ALLOW YOUR CHILD TO EXPERIENCE FAILURE.

Why would I say such a thing? Well, because without any struggle at all in life, there is no real way for a person to learn how to handle life when things are not picture-perfect. Think about the last thing that occurred that might not have been a positive experience. Did an appliance or vehicle ever break down at the worst possible moment? Ladies, perhaps your heel broke as you were walking into an important meeting. Think about the last negative thing that happened to you in your adult life. How do you initially react? Then, how did you solve the problem? Imagine if you were in this situation without ever having had to solve a problem independently.

How did you think this would have been different? For starters, you would not be able to think on your feet as quickly. Also, your emotions might begin to take over, leading to less rational thinking and less problem-solving. Do you think that learning how to solve your own problems as a child and young person might prepare you for the unexpected in life? I know—I ask a lot of questions. Take your time and go back to the beginning of this paragraph. Think about each answer before reading ahead. Remember, this is not a race. It is a journey, and it is meant to help you think deeply.

Without experiencing failure, the end result is a reward that may not be appreciated. Personally, I do not like cold weather. I am that person who wears a sweater to the beach. It's literally that bad. I have had several people share the adage that summer is often appreciated only because of winter. What does that even mean? It means that without the absence of warm weather, we cannot appreciate said warm weather. We need to be without to enjoy what we have to the fullest. Now, it's your turn. What is something you appreciate more when it is not there for a long time?

Can you think of a first experience you have had in life? Maybe you had to drive to an unfamiliar location for a doctor appointment or a new job out of state. What about the first time you drove a car, rode a bicycle with only two wheels, or attempted to learn a new skill? How was your first experience? Was it flawless and perfect, or was there something to be improved upon? Now, there might be a small group out there who can truthfully say these experiences were wonderful from the very beginning. If that is the case, then please consider your first crush, first date, or first breakup. Does that change things? If not, then congratulations to you. Now go buy a lottery ticket and shut up. I am only kidding ... about the lottery ticket, that is. Okay, for real this time; I was joking about the "shut up" part. A person that skilled and lucky must know the winning numbers.

I think back to when I learned how to drive. I never quite realized how big "I" was in a vehicle. I was no longer the length and width of my physical being. I had to take into account the passenger seat, the trunk, and the side mirrors as I flew down the highway with the wind in my ... nothing. I did not have a convertible. This new size meant parking took more than one swift maneuver. Who am I kidding? Parking now takes more than one swift maneuver. But it takes fewer maneuvers now than when I was eighteen years old. Notice I still am not using the word "swift" to describe them.

In addition, I was unable to drive more than seventy miles per hour in the very beginning without feeling as though I might lose control. It was almost as if I could feel the wind pushing the vehicle beyond my control. Today, that is not the case anymore; I can control the vehicle at any speed I drive—depending on the speed limit, of course—and with one or two hands on the steering wheel. In all honesty, I am a grandma behind the wheel; no adventurous speeding for me.

My prior experience with driving has taught me to handle more. This is also true with life experiences. Prior bad experiences prepare us to work through problems we have to solve without completely falling apart in a panic. Each time we come across something we need to tackle, it further prepares us for the road ahead into adulthood and our golden years. Isn't that what you want for your child? A life of independence, happiness, and fulfillment? Please help them get there when they need your guidance and life experience.

TIP #2: DO NOT BE AFRAID TO MAKE YOUR CHILD UNHAPPY.

Let this idea sink in just for a few seconds. Really give it some thought. Your child might be happy eating ice cream with whipped cream and a cherry on top for dinner three nights a week followed by chips and soda for dessert. While that will make your child happy in the moment, it will also make them physically sick and hurt their overall health. Now as a parent, is that what you are going to put on the dinner table to ensure your child is happy? Probably not. I hope not and if you do, I beg of you, please reconsider. Your child's happiness is not directly tied to their love for you, even if it feels that way now.

Your child may one day ask you why you made the choices and decisions you did for them when they were a child. When you were the adult and they were none the wiser. Will your parental choices stand the scrutiny of your child at eighteen years old? How about at twenty-five? What about the age when they have a child of their own and you become a grandparent for the first time? Time goes by quickly, and your children are young only once. Your child will continue to love you even when you say the dreaded word they wish did not exist—"no." Get used to that word, parents, because without that word, there is also no structure, routine, or, believe it or not, safety.

Boundaries for children create safety and security. They provide children with the knowledge they need in order to understand what might occur based on a choice they make. I'll share an example. I tell my child their room needs to be cleaned. If the room is not cleaned by the end of the day, then I get to keep their phone, iPad, or whatever else they treasure, even money. What motivates your child? What is important to them? Please evaluate those two questions before you continue down this path with your child.

Now what if it comes to the end of the day and the child has played video games all day, and the room is still a mess? What does a parent do? Should a parent beg and plead? While this may keep the child temporarily happy, you have now successfully taught this future adult that words mean nothing and there are no consequences for not doing what was asked. How does this transfer to adulthood? Once again, let's use your child's future boss as an example. Say they ask your child to complete a task, and it does not get done. Do you think the boss is going to keep your child on for much longer? Do you think losing a job and having no income is going to make your child happy? How about when they have to move back into their childhood bedroom? How might that affect their social or dating life?

Your job as a parent is to prepare your child to be successful and independent and, yes, happy. However, giving the world to your child on a silver platter will not ensure happiness forever. That happiness is fleeting. One last question here: Is this how you want to live your home life? I, personally, would prefer the joy and peace of a positive relationship with my children that will last until I die. I can die knowing my children can fend for themselves and be a positive influence on society and this country we love. Maybe they will even change my old-person diapers. A mom can dream.

Think about the friends you have. Do you ever ask for help? Do you help them when it's needed? Maybe you support each other without even asking. How do you think your child is ever going to make, and maintain, positive relationships if all they know is how to take rather than give? Do you envision your happy child lonely in life, or do you want your child to develop and have meaningful relationships, maybe even have some grandchildren at some point? Well, I'm not sure about you, but I would like to see my children with meaningful human connections and a happy marriage if that is what they want. It is our job as parents to ensure that our children are able to do this, and sometimes, that requires us to do and say things that might not make them happy in the moment. It will, however, set them up for future happiness.

Do you have more than one child? How do you think this type of family dynamic is going to work in this situation? If you do and give everything to your child or children, it is a one-way relationship in giving and taking. Yes, you might get some affection and love from your child, but it may be just so they can get away with something or gain something else. Now I am not saying this is absolutely the case, but it can be. In reality, it is more than likely a mix of emotions as well as wants and needs of the child. That would be for you to determine in each separate scenario and each individual child. Here is an example. Does your child give you a smile, hug, or kiss when they are asking for something?

Disclaimer: All children do this on occasion. You may want to consider how often this occurs and what the surrounding circumstances are in order to best determine if this is a regular behavior.

The concern here is: How do you think your children will feel and act toward each other? If both or all children are taught to take and not give, then what will they do to each other? That is the million-dollar question. It may be too scary to even answer honestly for some. If this question frightens you in any way at all, please make a change—it is not too late. Start building positive relationships and setting boundaries incrementally.

So, here is the big question. How will teaching your children to value and love others affect their current relationships and their future relationships as adults? I hope you would want to foster a positive and loving bond between your children. There is no doubt sibling relationships can be tricky. I often find that siblings are either very close or almost never speak to each other. Rarely did I come across something in between. When they travel through life, siblings should be the biggest supporters and most trustworthy confidants to each other. A sibling should be a constant source of positivity and support. To have a trusted and supportive sibling means you never have to walk through life alone. Isn't that what we all want? Partners and supporters through every age and stage of life?

CHAPTER 2

There Are Three Sides to Every Story

Think back to your favorite TV drama where the characters are in court. A witness gets up to testify on the stand and places their hand on the Bible. What comes out next? The individual states they plan on telling the truth, the whole truth, and nothing but the truth. Is that correct? In a perfect world, everyone would be honest all the time. In reality, people do not always tell the truth.

For students, sometimes being dishonest is an outright conscious choice, but often it is more complicated and can vary based on the age of the student. It would stand to reason that a fourth-grader would have a more accurate grasp of the situation than a first-grader would. Oftentimes, students are telling their version of the truth, which might not reflect complete accuracy to the actual situation. Students might remember just a few facts, or they might get mixed up completely if they are nervous or upset. This dates back to the dawn of the student. Bottom line is, if something does not sound right, check with your child's teacher. Please, one more time. Please verify with a different, trusted adult if your relationship with your child's teacher is in need of repair. Perhaps a teacher assistant, bus driver, or office personnel. Naturally, these are individual cases that are difficult to determine until you absolutely need to verify them. However, for the third time, please consult with a relevant adult any time you feel there is confusion on your end.

Some teachers joke that they promise not to believe everything a student says about what happens at home if you, as the parent, promise to do the same. What happens at home stays at home. Well ... sometimes not if you have a child with a mouth and some language skills. What that means is, if your child can talk, then they are spilling all the beans, and I do mean all the beans. Parents, we understand that students at any age talk about things that happen at home. If you have a child who can talk, you have no secrets from your child's teacher—I promise you. On more than one occasion, I have been told by a student that their parents' favorite beverage of choice was too much wine, beer, or other items in the category of twenty-one-and-over beverages. I have heard about when single parents date, married parents are going through a divorce, and some other embarrassing things I will not mention. If you are a teacher reading this, then you know exactly what I am saying. If you are a parent, then reverse it. You might be privy to the types of food your child's teacher likes, if they are dating or going through a divorce, or a favorite beverage. Parents, this does not mean your child's teacher goes around spilling personal stories to your child and the classroom. Children are perceptive and are learning what to say and not to say. I appreciate their innocence; they are not yet worldly enough to know what should be kept quiet. I like to enjoy the innocence; these days, it seems children lose it younger and younger.

Teachers do not hold these stories against parents and mostly realize that students, especially young students, might be confused. When teachers and parents have a cohesive relationship that focuses on the student, both sides get a big laugh about it. The upside here is that parents know just which type of wine to send to the teacher for a Christmas gift!

I'm only joking—that is not the moral to this story. Well, if it is a good Prosecco, then it possibly can be.

The moral of the story is good communication from both sides is key. The more adults work together, the better it will benefit the student at any age. While there may be some truth in what the students say about their homelives, teachers are aware enough to realize it's not the whole story. I see it this way: your child looks at their teacher as a trusted adult in their life, and you can respect that relationship by treating your child's teacher as well as your child would want. Here are some tips to help your child maneuver the classroom even though you are not there to observe.

TIP #1: LISTEN TO THE STORIES.
So, your child comes home from school, and you ask how their day went. Your child immediately flies into an animated story about what occurred on the playground, in the cafeteria, or even in the classroom. Insert the most interesting story your child has told you. Now, the first thing I ask my children is if they were directly involved. If the answer is "no," then I listen and enjoy the story. That is what it is, a story. I encourage my child to help another child in need if necessary but to not get involved in other people's drama.

Oh, you saw two classmates arguing over a pencil? That's nice. What happened? How did you help? Did you get an adult? Those are the questions I ask.

The types of questions and the way the conversation will go will vary on the age of the child. For example, if this situation involves my kindergarten child, I would encourage my child to get the teacher or teacher's assistant. But for my older child, I may ask if they had offered a pencil to the student who was without a pencil.

Each situation will be unique unto itself. The idea is to instill problem-solving and age-appropriate critical-thinking skills in your child in hopes it will not be your child grabbing a pencil from another child. Your child will already know that is not appropriate behavior.

This suggests that if we all teach our children the behavior is inappropriate, most will not do it. However, despite our best efforts to teach our children, the impulsivity of some youth can take over, and the pencil is grabbed before the child even knows it happened. That is a specific situation and not the context to which I am referring.

What if the answer to the question about being involved is a "yes" from my child? Now, what do I do? My child just told me a story where another classmate ripped the pencil right out of their hand while they were writing! It's terrible, awful, and something has to be done! All these words and emotions are filling your body and mind. What is your first reaction? Well, I encourage you to really listen to the story. Ask questions and ask for the story to be repeated, if necessary, to ensure you have heard all the gory details. Take a look at your child during this time. How are they? Are they laughing or crying? What do the body language and facial expressions tell you? You know your child. What you do not know is what exactly occurred with the children and the pencil.

What to do? The good news is you have options.

- You can race back to the school and demand the teacher explain.
- You can stew all night and give yourself an ulcer and possibly a panic attack thinking about this pencil-grabbing child.

- You can call the other parent and scream at them for raising a pencil grabber. You know your child already gave up the name.
- You can calmly send your child's teacher a message inquiring about the incident.

By the way, I highly discourage the first three options. While I know you are dying to do those things, they accomplish nothing. They just hurt your body, relationships, and possibly your health.

The fourth option allows you to begin to work on the situation and feel at ease. It also causes the teacher to address you in a calm tone and manner since it's how you addressed them when you gave them the information, thus building positive lines of communication and teaching your child the correct and appropriate way to handle certain situations like an adult.

TIP #2: PLEASE CONSIDER YOUR REACTION.

One thing to keep in mind is that your children are watching you. They are always watching you even when you think they are not. They use this knowledge in the real world. So, if you yell at your child to snatch back that pencil, well, that may be exactly what they do. When the real truth may not be that the other child was as aggressive as your child perceived or explained to you. Please consider what you have just taught your child. You gave them permission to use violence. Violence that might have escalated a situation. Violence that might be retaliated.

Please read this next part carefully. There is a clear difference in not allowing another student to grab the pencil. By that I mean, let's say the pencil-grabber tries it on your child. Your child should not allow their pencil to be grabbed, but they can prohibit the action in a calmer manner while being confident and assertive. This is different than being aggressive.

When you hear the story from your child, how do you react? Do you scream and jump around, or are you calm and quiet? I would advise you to allow your child the opportunity to tell the entire story prior to any sound effects or placed judgment. This means facial expressions should be kept neutral. No eye-rolling yet, parents. Save that for when your teenagers leave their dirty socks right beside the hamper or there is a stack of dirty dishes and cups on the floor near the door to their room.

Just kidding. Please keep the eye-rolling to yourself at all times.

This calm demeanor allows your child to tell the story as it occurred and not get confused, distracted, or caught up with your reactions. Your reaction also may have a hand in how your child handles this type of situation next time.

This means your child may enjoy telling these types of dramatic stories to get your attention. This does not mean your child made up the story. It just means there may have been a little more excitement added in. One of the best things about young children is the imagination, in my opinion. For example, it's possible the pencil grabber did not grab the pencil out of your child's hand while they were writing an epic piece of poetry that was forever lost. (How dare they!) No, in reality, the pencil may have been taken or even given in a more gentle approach.

What does this have to do with me, you ask? So glad you asked! As I mentioned earlier, your children are watching you. Always watching you. If you are looking to add spice and flare, well, that is great, but is this the time and place for that? Perhaps not.

TIP #3: PLEASE CONSIDER YOUR
CHILD'S PERCEPTION.

Back to the pencil grabber.

Your child may not have realized the entire event as it played out. They most likely were immersed in their own work or duties, and there may be an entire portion of the story that was left out, not purposefully.

Consider this scenario. It is an elementary classroom. Think kindergarten all the way up to the third grade. The students are working on an independent writing task, and the teacher informs the class it is time to clean up. Your child has one last word to write and rushes to get it completed. The student beside your child is a stickler for the rules and begins cleaning up immediately. This, unfortunately, includes the pencil in your child's hand.

Now, your child has just experienced a pencil being grabbed out of their hand. How might they interpret the story? Are they wrong when they make it sound worse than it was? Absolutely not! They are a child and sees things differently. Had you been a normal human being and not the Hulk—options one through three above, by the way—you might have been informed of the entire thing. What this means is: had you approached the teacher as suggested in option four above, you would likely have gotten the entire story calmly and professionally. Trust me, teachers see many things, and rarely are we surprised by the actions or behaviors of our students. This is even more true when a seasoned teacher has had the same grade level or age group for several consecutive years.

Now, scenario two. As you might know, many classrooms of all ages and stages have classroom helpers or jobs. Have you heard your child come home to proudly state they were the door holder, line leader, or paper passer outer? Yes, paper passer outer is a real classroom job. How do you think the class gets all their papers back? I have frequently seen students serve as pencil collectors. This eliminates pencils left all over the classroom or students not having a pencil to write with. Can you predict what I might say next? Yup, you got it. Your child was the victim of the class pencil collector.

Sorry, pencil grabber. I apologize. You were just doing your job.

I have seen both of these scenarios occur in real life as well as several other scenarios where a young student believed their pencil was grabbed from them. In reality, your child may have felt that their pencil was unjustly grabbed. If that is how your child feels, their feelings are completely justified. Children should not be told that their feelings are wrong, but the entirety of the situation should be clarified with the child. This can be done at home with the parent, at school with the teacher, or, ideally, in both locations to show the student that two of the most trusted adults in their life are united.

The point I am trying to make here is your reaction. Your reaction teaches your child how to react. Without all the facts, it may be challenging to provide good advice. I will typically give my child a few options on how to handle a similar situation if it happens again. For example, you can explain to your child that if someone grabs their pencil again, look at the person going for the pencil to see what they are doing. Are they collecting, helping, or just trying to grab? Then, act accordingly. This may mean doing one of the following: tell the other child you are not finished writing, get the teacher's attention, or simply take back the pencil. There are so many solutions that do not involve grabbing, pushing, or aggression in any manner. Then, after I calmly and humanely speak with my child's teacher, I can readjust my advice.

CHAPTER 3

Why Teachers Chose This Profession

Teaching, just like parenting, does not come with a manual.

Wouldn't that be nice and easy? Can someone write one please?

Students of any and all ages are often unpredictable to the point where they themselves do not always realize what they do or say at times. How many times have you heard your child—or maybe someone else's—blurt out something rude?

Why is that person wearing those shoes? Why do those fat people only have junk food in their grocery cart? Their hair is a mess!

They'll say these things really loudly in public and within earshot of said individuals with the terrible shoes, the messy hair, or the cart full of potato chips. Can you think of something else? I am cringing just thinking about what you might be recalling in your mind right now. Mortifying.

If that is the case at home, then why would it be so difficult to believe it happens at school? Take a minute and think about that. If you know your child embellishes at home, there is a strong chance it occurs in other locations. Where do children spend the majority of their time when not at home? School. So, it stands to reason that school is the place this might occur. Give it some thought.

Is there always beer or wine in your cup first thing in the morning? Well, I hope not, and if there is, then I ask that you rethink some decisions since your children know that, and you wouldn't want to teach them that habit. Of course, many of us enjoy a glass of wine or bottle of beer on the weekends and some evenings. That does not make us alcoholics. More often than not, on the Friday before Mother's Day weekend—and Father's Day weekend if your child is attending summer school or summer camp— your child's teacher will ask your child to draw a picture of you, and there is Dad in the backyard at the grill, holding a spatula in one hand and a beer in the other hand. Oops. Don't worry, parents. Teachers understand that this drawing is not an accurate depiction of your everyday life; they are not trying to send you to Alcoholics Anonymous meetings.

Sometimes, these moments make us laugh, but they can also help us bond. On most days—usually the first day of school—our students cry for you when you leave them at school and ask for you even as they progress through the elementary school grades. Your child loves you, and they need your support.

So, what does all that have to do with the reason teachers choose to teach? Well, I am glad you asked! Teachers have good intentions; however, the path is not straight. Rather, just as in parenting, the path is full of twists and turns. There is no yellow brick road, and no signs point to the closest exit. Teachers must overcome each obstacle and solve each problem as they come. They know this going in and make the choice to stay each year, until they don't—more to come on that later. Teachers choose this profession to help make their town, city, or state a better, more productive place where the next generation is able to become gainfully employed and independent. That is why teachers choose to teach.

I hope the next few tips shed some light into the mind of a teacher. I hope they help parents and teachers reconnect for the shared students in their lives. Please keep in mind that these are generalized and may not be the mindset of everyone. I would encourage both parents and teachers to actually find out what makes the teachers in their lives get out of bed every morning and teach their hearts out. Yes, teachers, you need to know that too. The knowledge will help you form bonds and work collectively together. When you take the time to make those valuable, personal connections, everyone is a winner, especially the students who are sitting in those classrooms and learning from every adult in sight.

TIP #1: IT'S FOR THE STUDENTS THEN AND NOW. Your child's teacher likely chose the profession and even grade level because they love children and learning—both lifelong lessons of their own and seeing their students learn—and want to help the youth of today become successful. While this may sound like a cliché, it is often the reality. For example, in my experience, the best language arts teachers love books, reading, and can edit the heck out of anything from a social media post to a dissertation without even blinking. They pass on that love to their students. Now this does not mean that students and teachers are always going to spend their days singing songs and holding hands around a campfire while rainbows and unicorns dance around the sky. Sometimes, teachers come across a problem. Everyone has problems at work; yes, that is true. Teachers celebrate the good days and leave the bad days behind to start fresh the next day. New day, clean slate for everyone. That's the rule.

Teachers choose this profession for the future of this country. Where would we be without teachers? How would students learn the needed skills for employment and life in general?

I have asked many teachers why they decided to join the profession. The overwhelming response was, "For the children." Schools today not only teach academics, but they also teach self-confidence, generosity, and so many other areas outside the realm of academia. They also provide some much-needed emotional support. Teachers are often seen by students and themselves as counselors, nurses, and many other things. Teachers believe in their students and work tirelessly to cultivate positive and productive members of society. I have known a small handful of teachers that could have retired but did not. They stayed to continue to support the younger generation. They stayed for the students and nothing else.

Most teachers enjoy the interaction with their students and love to see or hear when old students return to say hello. Want to put a smile on a teacher's face? Go back and visit one of your favorites. Speaking from personal experience, it is amazing to see and know that a former student is happy and successful. It also reaffirms that the teacher is making a difference. A quick visit from an old student is all a teacher needs to get through a bad day. What many may not realize is that teachers often spend a year teaching someone, only to never know where they land in life. Did they graduate high school, go to college, or perhaps join the military? Are they happy? Do they have children of their own? I would like to add here that these responses were not part of a formal interview. They were merely from coworkers discussing the job at the end of a long day.

In the world of technology, it is much easier to keep up relationships or find people. However, when your students are in the fifth grade, as an adult who is not the parent or a member of the family, it may be a challenge to know where the student ended up. As a teacher, it would not be appropriate to communicate with a former student who is still a minor. For example, I would not have a student as a friend on any of my social media accounts. So even with technology, I cannot reach out and see how they are doing.

I then asked the teachers why they stayed. The overwhelming response was, "For the children." Some of the teachers were high school teachers and they still felt that those teenagers needed support and guidance as they navigated into the real world of college, the military, or as part of the workforce. Students who have entered your classroom are always your students. To many teachers, once a child enters your classroom, they are your child, your kid, not simply a student. Have you heard the phrase, "Once a marine, always a marine"? The same applies here. Think of it like this: If your child goes away to college and no longer resides under your roof, are they no longer your children?

TIP #2: SOMETIMES, IT'S TO MAKE A DIFFERENCE.

Yes, this seems like something we say just to sound good. Well, I am sure some would do and say this with a lack of sincerity. However, for many teachers, making a difference is real. For the teachers who work in an area where most parents are not involved and food, resources, and money are scarce, teachers almost become parents to the students. Teachers are the most trusted adults when students have alcohol-

or drug-addicted parents or parents who do not know how to parent, so they check out. Teachers actually lose sleep worrying about their students.

If you go into any school and find a teacher who looks tired or worried, chances are they are not concerned for themselves. That tired teacher hasn't slept the previous night and quite possibly for more than that. What has this teacher so upset? One of their students would be my guess. More specifically, it is a student who is struggling, either academically or relating to something out of the teacher's control. This could be an academic struggle or something more out of the teacher's control. For example, it may be a child whom the teacher in question had to call child protective services for due to suspected abuse or neglect. It may be a child who never has any food or wears the same worn-out pair of pants each and every day. In either case, the teacher worries most for the child when they are not at school. They may wonder how the child is being treated, if they are hungry, or if the only hug they ever get is from the teacher. All of these ideas flow through the worried teacher's mind, and they cannot calm themselves until they set eyes on the child in need. They give the child one more hug as they exit the classroom at the end of the day. The teacher forces theirself to hold it together and hopes this child will find peace that night. Then tomorrow comes, and they do it all over again. As the years pass, the worried teacher does not stop worrying; they sometimes begin to see the signs sooner in their future kids. It never gets easier.

Academic struggles also cause teachers to worry. This worry is different, however, but does not give the teacher comfort either. At least this is something the teacher has some control over. The teacher can work to help their students. They can come to school early and stay late in order to work on lesson plans that will meet the struggling students' needs. They can also offer to tutor free of charge during those hours. They can ask for help from their colleagues. They can try one thing, and if it doesn't work, they can try another tactic. They do not give up. Rather, they give that student more of themselves.

Yes, helping students is their job, their duty. However, this teacher is a person too. They are an individual, likely with a spouse and a child or two. They are a person with thoughts, feelings, and desires. They are a person who takes their time from all those things to support your children. They deserve respect from their students, their students' parents, and the administration. They deserve to be greeted with a positive climate when they come to school each and every day. Think about it this way: If you were at a restaurant or a doctor's appointment, how would you treat the staff? When I say "staff," I am talking about everyone. At a school, the custodian should be given the same respect you give the principal. At any other establishment, the same rule applies. All people are equal. Anyway, I digress, let's get back to the restaurant. Would you yell and scream at your waitstaff? I hope not. I hope you would at least try to speak kindly to express your wants and needs.

Your opinion is valuable—that is undeniable. You are the parent, and teachers respect you as the primary caregiver and provider for their students. Teachers need you and your support. All the teachers would like is the same respect you give other professionals. Yes, teachers have a duty to help children that stretches past the hours of the school bell. That is not where the complaint is for most teachers.

TIP #3: THERE IS ALWAYS SOME GOOD.

Yes, a teacher's career has its challenges. So much so that when teachers tell other adults who are not teachers what they actually do for a living, the other adults often make a distressed facial expression. This horrified look is typically followed by an adamant comment about how they would never, and I mean never, do the job of a teacher. The age, subject, or grade level has no meaning. It's a hard "no." Usually, these other adults will continue with appreciation for their own children's teacher. This is the part I always like to hear. As a teacher, it never gets old hearing how other teachers and the profession itself are respected. The parents express the knowledge that their child likely drives his or her teacher crazy, and they try to make up for it with sweet and thoughtful holiday presents. Which, side note, is a considerate gesture but absolutely not necessary. I will say gifts are very much appreciated and some of the sweetest gifts have teachers smiling for weeks. My favorite gifts were the ones students made for me. I had one little first-grader paint me a handmade mug. I still have it and plan on keeping it forever.

While the profession has its challenges, each day is a new beginning and a new opportunity for greatness. This is something I've said before and will say again. Sometimes the greatness comes in the form of a kind note from a parent. Sometimes it is in the polite response of a student who says "thank you" when you smile and give a compliment. Sometimes it is simply in the way the students treat each other in the classroom and on the playground. Watching students interact in a positive manner always makes a good day. For teachers, it's the little things that count the most.

CHAPTER 4

Teachers (Time and Money)

Teaching is a tough gig. Students deserve a well-prepared teacher, which requires time and attention. The vast majority of teachers I have had the pleasure of working alongside are extremely hardworking, dedicated to their profession, and committed to their students. They work after hours, preparing lessons and talking to or emailing parents well into the evening and weekends. Yet, most teachers are forced to moonlight with at least one other side gig. Some tutor; some work or manage summer camps or after-school programs; and some choose to teach or work part-time online. Teachers in this country do not make enough to survive, yet they work tirelessly for their students.

What about the teachers who have kids of their own? When do they give them the time and attention they crave from their parents? After all, aren't they also students who may need help with their schoolwork? Being a working parent of any profession can be a challenge when it comes to balancing work and family, but when it comes to working as a single parent, the challenge grows exponentially.

Teachers as single parents find life challenging. Imagine having to pay rent, a mortgage, a car payment, all the other household bills, and possibly tuition for gymnastics, football, dance, or music lessons. This is, unfortunately, nearly impossible. We're talking about a profession that requires a four-year degree and encourages a master's degree for which many school districts do not pay tuition or offer a raise. Needless to say, this can be a frustrating experience for teachers. Teachers teach because they love it, but many leave because they cannot afford to live on the salary. (That may well be the saddest sentence in this book.)

Take a minute to consider the emotional well-being of your child's teacher. If you think a stressed-out teacher who can't make their rent or car payment has no bearing on your child, you are sadly mistaken. While your child's teacher may be well-prepared, organized, and kind, the underlying, chronic stress can weigh on anyone. Think about yourself. Imagine that each month you were not sure if you would be able to purchase groceries for your family.

Time out—what?! Teachers struggle to purchase basic necessities? The short answer is yes. I have known and actually been one of those teachers who are unable to purchase food, socks, or shoes for my own children and who worry about a possible dentist or veterinary bill that may be coming my way. Full disclosure here: I routinely have to tell my personal children, the ones I gave birth to, that they must tell me a few weeks in advance if they need something so I can budget it into my monthly check. A check I am grateful for from a profession that is meaningful and special. A profession that requires at least a four-year college degree and, oftentimes, a master's degree on top. A profession that also forces professional adults to seek part-time employment just to financially make ends meet. I know I'm repeating myself, but I want you to understand how difficult life can be for us teachers.

I will interject here that I am aware other professions face this same, sad situation. However, today, we are discussing teachers. The difference will become clear as you continue to read.

Let's go back for a minute. I would ask that you think about the importance of teachers in the classroom. Has your child or grandchild ever had a long-term substitute teacher? A long-term substitute teacher can teach temporarily if a teacher is on maternity leave or medical leave. This is not the type of situation I am referring to. I want to discuss long-term substitutes who fill vacant teaching positions at any point in the school year. Do you think your child is getting the same level of education when there is an individual who is not trained or experienced in teaching, as happens in some states? While long-term substitutes are basically saints in disguise—would you walk into a classroom of children without a lesson plan, without strategies for classroom management, and without the curriculum you will be teaching for an undetermined length of time? Teachers need to be paid as the professionals they are so they will be retained.

The question I pose is why are there so many teaching positions left vacant across the United States? Well, this comes down to three main concerns. They are working conditions, low pay, and attrition rates— don't worry, I will define these for you!

REASON #1: WORKING CONDITIONS
What are "teacher working conditions" anyway? I would ask that you think about other workplaces such as a doctor's office, bank, corporate office—you get it. Who pays for the supplies and needs of the employees? The business does. Well, while teachers do have access to some supplies, often each teacher and classroom has unique needs, and these needs alter each time the group of students change. Teachers repeatedly take their own money from their already-low salary to support their students' needs. Teachers are some of the most generous people I have had the pleasure to know. They are there because they want to be, but they still deserve a reasonable wage. They know the value of an effective teacher for student

success and what it can do for a child, classroom, generation, and society. What they do not have are things like petty cash or company credit cards, so they dig into their empty pockets and give more than they actually can.

Teachers, in some areas, are provided a means to express their concerns at the end of the school year in the form of a survey. This survey asks teachers if they are happy, how the principal and the students have treated them, and if they feel safe. One question even asks if teachers have been physically or verbally assaulted while on the job. This is used to help create better working conditions for teachers, yet, I have not seen the benefits at this point. On one survey, I specified that I did not feel safe and I had been physically assaulted. In fact, I was sexually assaulted. Guess what? Nothing ever changed. That is the problem. Districts and states need to focus on their most valuable resource. The humans. Which includes the student and the teacher. Let me ask you something: If a student was able to assault an adult, don't you think that same student can assault a classmate? Now, do I think the surveys should stop? Absolutely not. But someone needs to read them and make some policy updates. Hint, hint.

Did you know that each state has its own teaching license and requirements that coincide? This means that teachers, if they move to another state, must apply for a new teaching license, which takes time and money. Each state also has a set of exams that must be taken. Each exam is costly, and it takes weeks to get results back. One way to improve teaching conditions is to have a national license. Think about it. Didn't World War II occur exactly the same way regardless of whether I teach it to a fifth-grader in North Carolina or a fifth-grader in New York?

Working conditions also include the boss. In the case of a school, that means administration, otherwise known as the principal. Side note: If you are a burned-out teacher who became an administrator, I urge you to find another profession. Principals often began as teachers and then returned to school to move up the career ladder. While principals are the bosses of the building, in many public schools, they have rules of the state they must abide by, and there are often not many options or opportunities in decision-making. That is, the state creates and updates policies. Policy needs to reflect current needs of teachers and students. For example, schools do not set student-teacher ratios; that is a policy above the head of the school.

Better working conditions for teachers can only benefit students. Think about yourself as a parent. Aren't you a more effective parent if you are a happy parent? While the monetary cost of improved working conditions may be high, it will cost exponentially less in twenty years when the next generation is fully equipped to work in a global job market. When our American workforce is filled with a generation of productive members of society who are gainfully employed, ensuring their children have qualified teachers in every classroom, then we compete in the global economy by having a real education that can be used to get a good job and work toward something productive.

REASON #2: TEACHER PAY

This has been a hot topic in recent years. There have been protests and walkouts in districts over teacher pay. Teachers deserve a reasonable wage. Teachers work hard and earn it. More importantly, your children deserve it.

Did you know the latest research shows that teachers get better over time? Who knew practice made perfect?[1]

I am shocked.

Without teachers who stick around, students will not have quality instruction that prepares them for college and the workforce, not to mention life. Research also shows that the states with the lowest teacher salaries have the most teachers leaving the profession—known as teacher attrition rate.[2]

Food for thought: Would you rather have your child's teacher be fully devoted to and happy with the classroom and students, or would you prefer your child's teacher tired, overworked, and emotionally exhausted? I can say with certainty that I want my child's teacher to be devoted to the students and school without having to work another job. Teachers who are forced to work another job lose time for planning for the classroom. They also likely have more stress due to the increase in professional obligations and may even choose to permanently leave the teaching profession in favor of a more lucrative opportunity the second job presents. This now contributes to more quality teachers who have left the profession. Bottom line: once again, depending on your state, your child may be looking at a permanent substitute teacher rather than their trained and experienced classroom teacher.

The added stress put on teachers to work a second part-time job, tutor after school, or even work remotely can lead to fewer teachers coming into the profession. What I mean is this: Pretend for a minute that your sister, brother, parent, or friend is a teacher. Over dinner, coffee, or just conversation, you find out that the teacher in your life is stressed-out financially and cannot even go see a movie with you. Perhaps they have the funds to go to the movie but not the time since they work two jobs. Would you encourage your children to enter this profession? I can say with certainty that many teachers do not encourage their children to become teachers. In fact, teachers often discourage their own children from entering the profession. How is that for marketing? I think some public relations are in order.

Teachers are not looking to be rich. As mentioned several times over, most teachers are phenomenal human beings and love the students and the profession. This does not equate to a profession without problems or room for improvement. Teachers want to focus on the students—their whole reason for waking up each morning, planning and prepping each lesson—and go to work.

However, I pose this question: How can one individual be everything to their students when they are forced to focus their energy, thought, and time on a second job just so they can provide for their families?

Invest in your children and grandchildren. Invest in their present and in their future.

REASON #3: TEACHER ATTRITION

Let's start with the basics. Teacher attrition is when teachers leave the profession, and not all of them retire into their golden years and rocking chairs or to the golf course. Some of the teachers who leave the profession at a young age are trying to move on to other careers. The teacher attrition rate in the United States is high and climbing annually.[3]

The question parents might want to know is how teacher attrition affects their children. Here are some facts that might help with this question:

- A reduction in the teacher attrition rate by half can almost eliminate the teacher shortage this country is facing.[4]
- Teachers are the number one influence on student achievement.[5]
- About 90 percent of open teaching positions are due to teacher attrition, most of which are teachers who leave the classroom prematurely. Who do you think fills these positions? Possibly a qualified teacher, but maybe it will be a long-term substitute teacher. Think about the law of supply and demand.[6]

Data from the National Center for Education Statistics Schools and Staffing report provides eye-opening information that will have long-term effects for our children and grandchildren if the current trends continue. There are more teachers leaving the profession than are coming in.[7] There are also fewer college students sitting in educational programs. This means there are even fewer students going into teaching. According to current research, about 8 percent of teachers leave the profession annually. The majority of this percentage is not due to retirement—that is about 3 percent annually.[8,9] While the supply of teachers is going down, this, undoubtedly, is a huge concern for the future of our children in the country. However, that is just half the problem.

While the first half of the problem focuses on the decline of the supply of trained and educated teachers, the second part of the problem is the increasing demand, or need, of these qualified teachers. Current data reflects that teacher demand is on the rise and does not seem to be stalling anytime soon.[10] If you are interested in reading the entire 107-page report, it is available for public access.

So, what does this even mean? This means fewer teachers and more students, which can turn into larger class sizes with less attention given to your child or grandchild. It can also mean your child or grandchild, depending on where you live, will be taught by an unqualified and unlicensed adult. Notice I did not say teacher. A teacher is an individual with a teaching degree, not a long-term substitute. Although, substitutes are Good Samaritans and should be well-valued members of any school. Teachers are human and do get sick from time to time. I would ask that you think about the quality of education your child's teacher can provide. Now think about if there was a substitute teacher. Which individual does the class respond to more? Who can provide lesson plans and classroom management? Last question, I promise: Who do you want in your child or grandchild's classroom?

One important thing to consider here is the emotional well-being of your child's teacher. Your child's teacher is often not just an academic instructor. Your child's teacher spends their days wearing the hats of counselor, nurse, mediator, and overall problem-solver. Imagine the stress of all this multitasking. Now, imagine it with zero support from anywhere. How can one person be all these things without anyone lifting them up? Teachers give so much and deserve support for themselves, which can be as simple as recognizing when the teacher has done something unique, such as checking on a student who is in the hospital for some reason or sick at home. Recognition can come from both parents and administrators also. When was the last time you said a kind word to your child's teacher, complimented them, or even thanked them for helping your child? If you do this already, great! If not, I would urge anyone to take the first step and write a note or send an email. Help provide the positive support that will build up your child's teacher.

Here is the question for the chapter: How can the United States reduce teacher attrition rate to ensure that all classrooms and students have access to trained teaching professionals? In a few thoughts, teachers deserve a reasonable wage. One that meets the needs of the teachers, such as purchasing groceries weekly and paying the rent on time, without them having to work a second job. Teachers need the support of parents and administrators when it comes to classroom needs. Teachers also need to be treated as well as other professionals are treated. This last one may not apply to every district, but if this is the case in yours, then please have some faith in your teachers.

CHAPTER 5

Ineffective Teachers

Just like cheating spouses and aggressive dogs, ineffective teachers do not speak for the majority of the professionals teaching. However, they bark the loudest and are often the most attention grabbing.

Take a look at scenario one. You take your car to the mechanic to be fixed and when you return later in the day, your car runs well. No problem. You politely thank the mechanic, pay the inflated bill, and drive home quiet and content. No need for barking.

Now, scenario two. When you retrieve your car in this situation, the problem has not been corrected. How do you handle this? Do you ignore the broken-down car you just paid to be fixed? Do you take it somewhere else and pay again to have the same problem corrected?

Which scenario barks louder? I am going to assume you picked scenario number two. If you did not, then you know what happens when you assume something. That is now me. I can admit defeat; it's okay. However, I would ask that you take a moment or longer to please contemplate which scenario was helpful. Was it the one that barked louder? As you continue to read, keep this scenario in the back of your mind. That is all I ask. At the end, if you are angry with me, then tell me. I welcome ideas I agree with and those I do not.

Some of the most outstanding teachers are structured, well-organized, and no-nonsense. There is a fine line between this individual—insert teacher name who comes to mind here—and the grumpy teacher who sits behind the desk, never budging an inch even in the most dire of circumstances. I will interject these thoughts: The purpose of school is to learn, and it is challenging to be a student, parent, or teacher in this world. Please do not mix a structured teacher who pushes your child to the fullest potential with a teacher overdue on retirement. These statements can be applied to the young as well. It's all in the mind and spirit. Here are a few tips I've put together for your toolbox of strategies that will help foster relationships and build a positive climate if you find yourself in this predicament.

TIP #1: YOU DON'T HAVE TO GO HOME, BUT DON'T COME TO SCHOOL EITHER—THIS TIP IS FOR THE TEACHERS.

If you are unhappy about the mere thought of school when you get up in the morning, then maybe teaching is not for you. Teachers, I know this is often a thankless profession, much like parenting can be at times, and I can completely empathize with you. However, you are doing nobody any favors by showing up simply to collect a paycheck or because you are too lazy to look for other employment opportunities. You are not only hurting your students, but you are adding, or, dare I say, even causing, a potentially toxic work environment depending on how many others you want to bring down with you in your bad mood.

In the end, you are sacrificing your very own happiness, and I would assume—don't worry, I haven't forgotten what this makes me if I'm wrong— most people would not care to stay in a workplace that is not the right fit. Why not do everyone a favor, including yourself, and find a job you enjoy that makes you smile when you get up in the morning? None of us are getting any younger, and the more time passes, the more difficult this becomes. Retirement from teaching can come at any age.

What if you are a young teacher and realize quickly the profession is not for you? Well, you have more options than teachers who realize this when they are much older. You have the time to go back to school if a new career piques your interest. Perhaps you could even move somewhere else because the town, city, or even state is not for you. New job, new town, new you. Just go for it.

TIP #2: THERE IS KNOWLEDGE TO BE GAINED HERE—THIS TIP IS FOR THE PARENTS.

Think of this as a learning opportunity for your child as well as for yourself. Think about your place of employment, the gym you go to—or try to anyway—or even large family gatherings. Do you like and respect everyone in all these situations? Probably not. However, you are an adult, and if you want to keep your paycheck, remain unbanned from public places you may wish to visit in the future, and prohibit your family from witnessing the side of you you hope never is exposed, you keep these negative feelings to yourself. No one ever said you cannot think them. Those thoughts are for your mind only. I would caution this practice just a little, as lingering thoughts can have the potential to seep in and may lead to stronger negative feelings, which can spiral into negative action we just decided was not proper adult behavior to be exhibited in life. If your negative thoughts run away with you, you might want to seek the expert advice of a counselor or therapist to talk them out. Just a suggestion.

One thing I may ask myself is this: How can I learn from the situation? How can this, in any way, provide a life lesson for my child or even me? After all, we are all improving and evolving. Those processes don't stop when we reach adulthood. Well, the answers may surprise you, or, after reading the previous paragraph, maybe you already have an idea of what is coming next. This situation prepares students to have patience, exposes them to various personalities, and shows them what it is like to work with someone with whom they may not agree.

Think of it like this: Your child graduates and continues on to gainful employment in their desired field. Their life is amazing. Every parent's dream. However, as an adult, they come into contact with a coworker, possibly even a boss, who clashes with their personality. Your adult child is not prepared to handle this situation with grace. Now that is a general statement, and there are plenty of individuals who have only experienced stellar educators and yet are unable to communicate with difficult people. Example number two: prior to that perfect employment, your child had an unsavory professor, one who reminded you of the teacher who was described above.

My advice is simple. Always maintain your composure and be the bigger person. I know that is a tough order to fill, but I encourage you to try it this way. For the sake of your children, at least try. Keep in mind that your child is watching you and hanging on to every nasty word you say about this teacher. What is that behavior going to teach your child? Nothing good, I would imagine. I would even go so far as to say that your reaction will teach them far more than this one individual who is a fleeting moment in your child's life. You are there every day as a role model. So keep your cool even when you're hot with anger. If it is a teacher your child will only have for a year, this will all be ancient history sooner than you may think. Although, I would say something to the administrators in the building and would not recommend that you stay completely quiet. I would recommend that you consider how you handle this situation as well.

Now, on to administration. Talking to them can be done over the phone, but meeting in person may be your best option. There are so many nonverbal cues such as body language and facial expressions that are missed when the conference is on the phone. I would also request that the teacher be present. In this manner, you are not meeting in order to speak poorly about another person but rather to discuss your difference of opinions with the person. This next part I cannot stress enough. Allow the teacher to respond to your questions and to speak. This is not an I-am-the-parent-and-I-am-always-right" situation. That kind of attitude will get you nowhere and will not solve a thing. Remember, this individual spends hours a day with your child, and it is in the child's best interest for the adults to work things out. Please have an open mind, but be sure to express your opinions, thoughts, and feelings. The purpose of this meeting is to hopefully come to a mutual understanding, not to be mistaken for a mutual agreement. At this point, there are two possible scenarios. One is that all the adults remained polite adults, and at the very least, compromises were made in the best interest of the students—and not just your child. However, there is a possibility this meeting did not go well. So as a parent, what happens next?

TIP # 3: HOW DO I INTERACT WITH MY CHILD'S TEACHER IF I DO NOT AGREE WITH THEM?

This is where it can get tricky. As a parent, the first thing I may want to do is yank my kid out of the school in a blaze of glory. However, I would caution you to consider your options first. While the situation may not be ideal, think about your what child wants and not what you want. Here is a short checklist of questions you should ask yourself if you are not completely sure:

- Is my child happy?
- Is my child successful?
- Is my child struggling academically?
- Does my child have friends?
- Is this a permanent situation?
- What are my other options for educating my child?
- What does my child want?

After careful consideration, it is time to make a choice. Just remember that your choice will affect your child the most and no one else. Please proceed with caution. I know—I do say that often—but caution makes us stop and think without rushing to action. I sometimes find a student in my office who has done or said something impulsive. Their response is usually along the lines of, "Well, I didn't actually mean to do or say what I just did or said. It just came out, or I just did it." That is when I tell them that sometimes, our bodies, mouths included, act before our brains are ready. We need to make sure we think everything through before we make another mistake. That is self-control. Something many of us adults can use a bit more of.

CHAPTER 6

Message to Parents

First, I would like to thank all the devoted parents who put their children first on the priority scale. As teachers, one of the most unfortunate and difficult parts of the day includes watching children come to school without weather-appropriate clothing or something to eat. Some of them may also have bruises or invisible scars from abuse, which is heartbreaking to see. If you are a parent who loves and respects your child, you are doing a great job, and teachers can see that in your child on a daily basis. Once again, thank you. While treating your child with respect and dignity will not eliminate problems for your child, it provides a loving and supportive place to work through them as well as the coping skills to problem solve.

Parents are often referred to as a child's first teacher. After all, a parent might have five years with a child before any teacher is introduced to the child. Parents ensure that children are prepared for their day at school. Parents wake up their children, feed them, dress them, and then actually get them to the building. For some, those are no small feats. Then, there is after school. Parents help with homework, feed them, bathe them, and then take care of the bedtime routine. I hope this includes reading to your child or having them read to you. That bonding time is precious and can never be brought back. It builds an emotional connection and a love of reading. Both will help your child begin life and school on a positive note. As a parent, you have the opportunity to start your children off with the best in life.

In a perfect world, parents, teachers, and students would all work together in perfect harmony. However, the reality looks quite different. The reality is none of the three parties is completely innocent at all times. Sometimes it is the parent who is in the wrong; sometimes it is the student; and sometimes it is the teacher. Each situation is different and should be handled as such. Please do not hold a grudge with your child's teacher simply because you had a problem with a different teacher last year. Each teacher is different and deserves the opportunity to begin fresh. Just as students get a clean slate daily, so should your child's teacher.

Below, I have shared some of the more common concerns I see between parents and teachers and possible ways in which you have the power to maintain a positive relationship. Please keep in mind that your child's teacher spends several hours a day with your child. This is an important relationship for your child. As the second adult in the parent and teacher relationship, I would ask that you please read the next section with an open mind. Once again, please remember that your children are watching you and emulating your words and actions. What do you want them to take away and learn from you?

TIP #1: HOW TO CRAFT A WRITTEN RESPONSE WHEN ANGRY.

Have you ever been upset or even angry with your child's teacher? While I wish this were never the case, I know all too well that it is not only an occurrence but also a common one. Have you stopped to consider why you are feeling this way? Do you have all the facts? Think of this time in a positive light and begin your investigation with your child's teacher. Go straight to the source. I can guarantee the person who spends the most time with your child and was the actual witness knows more than administration, who would only repeat what the classroom teacher has expressed. Why not get it straight from the horse's mouth? My inclination is to think that, when angry, mama or papa bear take over and emotions rather than logic rule and make you want to go for the highest in the building's chain of command. However, if you stop and think, will that accomplish anything? Will you get what you need? Chances are you will blow off some steam and possibly feel better in the moment, but at what price? I can tell you it will cost you your reputation in the school community, your integrity, and quite possibly your relationship with the individual at the other end of your tongue lashing if there were witnesses.

When you are experiencing any type of negative feeling, take the advice from a very wise third-grader I have had the pleasure of speaking with: count backward, take a deep breath, and stop before you say anything. My advice to add to this wise student would be to sit down and compose an email or message to the teacher. Do not hit send right away! Please, please have some self-control. If you feel you are on the impulsive side, then ask your spouse, significant other, or anyone nearby to keep your device away from you until you have a cool head. Walk away and then read the message again. Perhaps triple-check it just in case you called the recipient a joker, fool, or clown. Make sure you will be able to show your face at the next school event if it accidentally gets sent. That's the goal.

Once you are satisfied, go ahead and send the message. This is where you must wait patiently for a reply. If you send your message long after school hours, you may not get a response that evening. This does not mean your child's teacher is lazy or uninterested. It simply means they are taking care of their family and that time needs to be respected as well. You are an adult; be patient. If you do get a response, please keep in mind what I just wrote—this is the personal time for the other adult. Please make every attempt to use a respectful tone and language as you craft your response. This will help to continue positive communication.

TIP #2: HOW TO CRAFT A VERBAL RESPONSE WHEN ANGRY.

I can start with absolute certainty here. Threatening to call the news or blast on social media is not the best way to bond with your child's teacher or get what you and your child need. Start off with a smile and ask how you can help your child and then follow through. I would also encourage you to speak up for what you feel your child needs in a respectful and professional manner, of course. If you are on the phone, smiling can still work. It can give you a physical reminder to speak positively and be kind. Keep your objective in mind, which I hope is to help your child.

The phone can be a bit more challenging, as I mentioned previously, since you cannot see facial expressions or body language. It may also be difficult to discern when the other party has finished speaking and when would be the appropriate time for you to begin speaking. I would ask that you try to take turns so everyone has an opportunity to voice concerns and explain themselves. Speak clearly and ask questions. Be direct but nonconfrontational.

Remember your mission here: to come to a mutual understanding and, hopefully, a solution to the reason you are angry. Listen when it is the teacher's time to speak and answer the questions asked of you as well. I am confident that if you are kind, then your child's teacher will be kind as well. At the end of the conversation, if you are not satisfied, please refer back to chapter five, in which I discuss effective teachers and how to best handle the situation. Here is a checklist that may come in handy:

- Use your voice reserved for professional situations; think of it as practice for when you might meet the Queen of England or your favorite idol—who knows?
- Keep the turn-taking even and steady.
- Listen actively.
- Explain why you are upset in full details.
- Suggest a follow-up time in the future to revisit the situation (if applicable) to gauge the effectiveness of the decisions made.

TIP #3: HOW TO HELP YOUR CHILD AT HOME.

Many of us are parents. We have multiple children and each one is a little bit different in personality and behaviors. These differences may lead us to treat each one in accordance with their particular needs. This is called "being fair." It works in the classroom and at home. In both cases, structure is the best practice. The best way to help your child with schoolwork is to help them if needed. In the lower grades, please at least check homework or check in with your child. This goes back to what I just wrote about fairness. One of your children may not need anything but your signature, while another may need you to sit at the table with them in the seventh grade. Neither is wrong.

What does your child need? Just be honest with yourself, your child, and your child's teacher. Please do not tell your child's teacher you read with your child nightly when, in fact, you do not. This will only serve to hinder the academic progress of your child. It will not hurt your child's teacher. Your child is the victim in this charade to save face and appear as a supportive parent in the eyes of the school. Honesty really is the best policy here.

If your child has a poor or failing grade, that is on the student, not the teacher. Think back to the last time you saw a report card from your child or children. For those parents who saw their child was making a C or less, with whom did you immediately get upset? Was it your child? If that is the case, then congratulations. You are raising your children to be accountable and responsible. I applaud you. I see success and happiness in your child's future. However, if your first inclination is to be angry, hurt, or frustrated with the teacher, then I would encourage you to rethink that line of logic.

There used to be a time when children feared poor grades. Now, it is all too common for the teacher to be treated as the villain when a student earns a failing grade. If you have not already picked up on my words, please take note here. I said that students *earn* failing grades. They are not given. They are earned. Earned through the students' actions, participation, or failure to complete the assignment tasked to them. Either way, failing grades are earned by the student.

When failing grades are earned by the student, I would highly encourage a healthy conversation with your child and then with both the teacher and child in a student-led conference to determine how the child needs to be supported. If the child is too young for a student-led conference, then a regular parent-teacher conference will work just as well. There is no one-size-fits-all answer here other than to communicate in a positive nature. The takeaway is this: the child must take responsibility for the grade and must not blame or shame the child's teacher. Parents, if you take one thing away from this chapter, please consider this one more time. Students, not teachers, earn failing grades. I think this warrants reiteration. Students, not teachers, earn failing grades.

There is one more thing I would like to stress to parents. Your child's teacher works with your child for several hours a day. We already know your child isn't perfect. Who is? Coming to a conference thinking the teacher is wrong and the student is correct may lead to conflict. Open your mind and be honest. Tell your child's teachers that while you understand your child is not perfect, you expect your child to be taken care of and respected during school hours. This does not mean your child gets to do and say anything they want. However, mutual lines of communication and respect are vital to all included, even if they are not old enough to drive, join the military, vote, or purchase an alcoholic beverage. Children deserve and should be given the proper respect at all times.

TIP #4: IT'S JUST LUNCH, OR IS IT?

How many of you think about what your child eats every day while in school? Do you provide a snack, or does your child take a lunch you pack for them? If your child eats breakfast or lunch (or both) at school, than this next section should rightfully be called, "It's just dinner, or is it?" Perhaps the word "dinner" can be replaced with an after-school snack. Either way, when you have control over your child's nutrition, what they eat should be taken seriously. Notice I used the word "nutrition" and not "meal." Nutrition is what fuels your child's brain. It provides the fuel for cognitive reasoning and allows your student to remain focused on learning.

Now, let's talk about what is inside the lunchbox. Have you heard the expression "you are what you eat"? Different foods react differently in the body. Your student is growing and developing each passing day. Don't you want to give your child the best chance for optimal performance? Food can be your solution. Food can be one of the simplest things to change, and one you have the most control over. When parents come to me for advice when their child is struggling, one of the first things I ask is, "What does the child eat? Are there cookies, candies, and processed foods, or are there fruits, vegetables, and fiber?" While the latter may not be the most fun, they are the best for your child's development. If you do an internet search asking about the benefits of these items for children, you will likely come across pages and pages that explain fruits and vegetables supply the body with much-needed vitamins, minerals, fiber, and water.[11] As children grow, healthy eating can lead to lower risk of chronic diseases such as high blood pressure, high cholesterol, and type 2 diabetes, which are becoming all too common in children.[12] I am definitely not saying to never eat cakes, cookies, or doughnuts (the horror!); just do not eat them every day. Also, do not eat them as your morning snack at school.

Eating too much sugar can affect the brain and lead to loss of focus, poor memory, hyperactivity, and moodiness.[13] None of these things sound as if they would help your child learn to read, write, or be happy. Think about the sugar crash. It's not good, and it's definitely not good for a student at school to experience that feeling. If the end goal is happiness for your child, why would you continue to provide these food items to them? Now is a doughnut just a doughnut? I think not.

Well, I have said a mouthful, but I don't expect you to just take my word for it. After all, I am not a doctor who gets to wear the oh-so-fashionable white coat. I am simply an individual who has done the research and observed the side effects in classrooms. According to researchers from Harvard University, Cleveland Clinic, Mayo Clinic, *Psychology Today*, and Autism Speaks, nutrition and food choice can play a larger role than you may anticipate in things such as mood, anxiety, and the ability to focus while in the classroom.[14] The right food supplies your child's body and brain with vitamins and antioxidants to repair and replenish themselves.[15]

Have you had your own parents and grandparents tell you to eat your vegetables? What did they know that this modern world has forgotten or maybe not realized yet? Current research shows that green vegetables like spinach, broccoli, and leafy greens can slow cognitive decline.[16] It isn't just the green veggies either. According to several research studies, an assortment of fresh vegetables is a vital staple needed for children. Berries are some of the best examples; they help improve memory and are loaded with antioxidants, which have healing properties. In other words, memory and thinking can be preserved for longer periods of time.[17]

Fruits and vegetables will make your child happy and successful, both in body and spirit. Foods that do the opposite are the processed junk foods such as chips, cookies, and most anything else you can find in those aisles at the grocery store. Once again, these items in moderation, combined with lots of healthy choice foods, are what I am suggesting here.

Think about this. Have you really considered what ingredients are in a bag of chips? There are artificial colors and flavors that comprise the bulk of the ingredients list. What is an artificial color or flavor anyway? Something created in a lab and not a natural food grown for human consumption, that's what.

Picture this scenario in the school cafeteria:

"What do you have for lunch?" Megan asked her third-grade classmate from across the cafeteria table.

"Well," said Sara, "I have a bag of artificial colors and flavors, and it tastes so good!"

Hmm, somehow I cannot picture that actually happening. How about you?

Does a cheese puff grow on trees or in the ground? Does it come from nature in some other form such as mother's milk? No, it does not. Not only that, have you considered what these artificial ingredients may do to us? According to current research, these artificial ingredients have been linked to the inability of children to remain focused in school as well as hyperactivity. This is sometimes referred to as brain fog and it is exactly what its name suggests. Brain fog occurs when the body does not get proper nutrition and leads to poor concentration and memory. Some of this is due to the amount of added sugar in these processed foods. Further explanation is to come.[18]

So what exactly is added sugar? Before you say anything—yes, fruit has sugar. But rather than added sugar, fruit contains natural sugar. Unless you purchase the fruit in a pouch or cup, or can. Then you will need to check the label to verify if sugar has been added. Added sugar is sugar companies put into your food to alter the taste. It has many names and is often hiding in foods we deem "healthy," so I encourage you to do your own research and read labels. Now, what does this added sugar do to your child? Added sugar can affect the brain and lead to issues with memory.[19]

Memory issues in school can cause challenges with learning. Consider how this may affect your child in math class. The addition and subtraction learned in one grade level is needed as a committed memory to aid your child when learning how to multiply in the next grade level and then to divide in the next grade level. Do you remember learning your multiplication tables? How difficult do you think it will be to pass these classes without a fully functioning memory system in your brain?

What I am referring to is not a quick fix. You can't just simply put an apple instead of a bag of chips in your child's lunchbox for a few days so the teacher will get off your back and you will look like a caring parent. What I am suggesting is to baby step your way to healthy eating, for both you and your children. If you were to go on a diet and decide you are going to eat cabbage soup or a juice cleanse for a week, wouldn't it be less painful with family support? Imagine being a child who is given an apple, knowing full well that you, the parent, are not eating apples at all. You are eating chips, doughnuts, and ice cream. How successful do you think that would end for anyone? If you are thinking not so much, then yup, I concur.

The best way to start is with one item. Once eating that is a habit, then bring in another. An idea, if you are looking for one, may be to start with reducing the amount of added sugar in your family's diet. The idea is that added sugar can be consumed but not in excess. All right, let me address the definition of the word "excess." What does it mean? Should I eat one doughnut instead of two for breakfast? Or possibly never eat a doughnut again? The answer is neither. Think of excess sugar as a daily thing in the beginning and work from there. If you look up the dietary guidelines from the U.S. Department of Health and Human Services, you will find they recommend added sugars be less than 10 percent of total food intake for the day. This includes sugar-sweetened drinks. The guidelines recommended here are no more than eight ounces a week. Yes, you read that correctly. Only one small cup of sugar-sweetened juice per week, not per day or per meal.[20] Wow! Did I also mention that added sugars have absolutely no nutritional value? So what do the guidelines say about what I should be feeding my child? The guidelines recommend eating fruits and vegetables regularly.[21] This means daily, and it means both fruit and vegetables, not one or the other. As for sugar, the guidelines state that if your child is between the ages of two and eighteen, less than six teaspoons of added sugar a day should be ingested.[22]

One question I asked myself a long time ago when I began my own personal journey toward understanding what is considered healthy eating was, Just how bad is added sugar for your body and your child's body? Here are some answers I have discovered in my research. If you or your child fill up on junk, there is no room for the nutrient-dense food. What I mean is this: I just ate an entire pizza with extra cheese, so do I really want to eat a salad? The sad truth is no, I do not, and neither will my child. Maybe we should eat the salad first and then eat the pizza. That is a start to making a change.

What else can I do, you ask? Well, I happen to have some suggestions up my sleeve just waiting for you!

How about adding some fiber to your family's diet? This will provide your stomachs and brains with the needed nutrition and also fill you up so you may be less inclined to reach for the processed junk in the pantry or freezer. Perhaps next time you are at the grocery store, you do not purchase anything from the frozen section such as dinners, pizza, or other junk. I know—that may be too big of a step. Take your time. Try buying less and less until less turns into none. You may surprise yourself. Your taste buds may decide they no longer crave this type of food.

Here is some food for thought. Added sugars (in excess) reduce the production of a brain chemical called brain-derived neurotrophic. Now, you may want to know why you should care about this chemical. You should care about it because without it, a student's brain struggles to form new memories.[23] Think back to my scenario in math class. How can a child learn to divide if they are unable to maintain the memory of their multiplication facts?

Look, the truth of the matter is that you are not alone, and this is certainly not easy. Parenting is a challenge. It does not come with a manual, and every child is different. You can only do your best each and every day. Sometimes you will see success and other times not so much. The beauty is each day you get to start fresh.

One thing I have always told my students is that we do not hold grudges. Maybe you didn't make a good choice yesterday, and today you are standing in the doorway worried I will be angry with you about it. That will not happen. Instead, I will absolutely greet you with a smile and not mention the previous day. Move on and try again. I tell the students that mistakes are never mistakes if you learned something. Sometimes the same mistake does occur, and that is all right also. The intent of doing right needs to be a focus, and you also need to bring forth your absolute best effort to meet the good intention. That is what I ask of my students, and that is what I expect from them as well as from myself. Lead by example.

TIP #5: WILL HOMESCHOOLING TURN MY CHILD INTO AN ANTISOCIAL OUTCAST?

The answer to this question is a big N-O, no. Your child has a personality you can foster and inspire to greatness even without classroom peers. Actually, without the schedule of a classroom, you can foster the passions of your child to a greater extent. Perhaps your child would like to learn how to play an instrument or loves to create art. Your day is just that, yours. To plan, travel, and make the best of. Once again, you should do what you feel is best for your child. Homeschooling is a personal choice.

In my experience, many teachers have not supported homeschooling in the general sense. This lack of support is due to the rigor of the state curriculums. However, each state has its own standards, with some states lagging behind others. This can be problematic for transient students such as those who relocate because a parent experiences a job change or a permanent change of station in the military.

Based on what I have seen and heard, homeschooled students often have to repeat a grade due to the fact that they have not had exposure to the entirety of the curriculum. Then, if and when they return to traditional school, they are often unable to maintain an academic pace in the classroom. This is absolutely not due to the intelligence level of the child; it comes down to the amount of material covered in the classroom versus the amount of material typically covered by a parent at home. In my humble opinion, this is due to the parent not knowing exactly what they need to teach their child at home as it pertains to academics. This is not related to the intelligence level of the homeschooling parent or even desire to teach the child at home. As I stated before, teaching is a profession that requires years of education and student teaching experience.

A good question to ask is, "Should I homeschool my child?" I have had several parents ask me about homeschool options. What do I think? My response is this: If you are comfortable with the academic material, then please feel free to homeschool. If you feel your child needs one-on-one attention or the traditional classroom is not the right fit, then maybe this option should be explored.

Today, there are several options for parents and students, and choosing to homeschool does not have to be a permanent situation. Your child possibly has special needs that require more specialized attention than you can provide, so homeschooling may be a viable option. My best advice is to seriously consider the time and attention you must put into this. Homeschool is not an excuse to sleep all day, play video games, and not learn. If you choose to homeschool, please take it seriously.

The second most asked question refers to socialization. My advice here is that school is not a place just for socializing. It is an institution for learning. Now, I will add that school does teach students more than academics. Students learn to take turns, wait in line, and adapt to new things. All great for proper social skills. My argument is that social skills can be learned in other places. If you would like to homeschool but are worried about socializing, consider these options. You can join a local homeschool community group. Usually, these groups meet to go on field trips or just to socialize. Parents can register their children for sports, clubs, or other extracurricular activities. These activities will involve the same socialization skills your child will see at school. Bottom line, homeschool is a good option for some, but you have to put in the work to do it properly. If you do not, your child is the one who will be unprepared for life as an adult.

I would caution you to consider all options prior to making this choice. Is homeschooling something you are comfortable with? Is it something your child wants to do? If the answer to both of these questions is yes, then the next step may be to talk to local parents about homeschool and delve into the material.

If you are going to homeschool, one piece of advice I always provide is to create and maintain a schedule. This is the way to ensure that your child may be able to return to the traditional classroom if needed without too much of a disruption or shock. As well, it prepares your child for life in the real world, as I can almost guarantee that gainful employment will have a regular schedule.

Now this does not mean you need to wake up, have lessons, recess, lunch and then an extra class such as gym, music, or art. It simply means you create a schedule that works for you and your child. Depending on the age of your child, you may want to include them in the creation of the schedule to give them personal accountability. The more the student is included in decision-making, the more personal it is. Homeschooling looks different for everyone; please keep this in mind. Homeschooling is a personalized education.

TIP # 6: THE POWER SCHOOLS DO NOT HAVE.

Schools can do many things. Schools can teach academics, create friendships and bonds with others, and prepare students for the next steps in their lives. However, schools today have lost much of their authority.

Picture it: Your child is sitting in a classroom with another student who constantly does not follow directions. This child sits directly behind your child. Let's call this child John. John decides to pull your child's hair, take food out of another student's lunch box, and walks around the classroom whenever they want to. Distracting, isn't it? Each time the teacher has to address John's behaviors, your child has lost that instructional time. The teacher may be able to ignore some of the behaviors, but do you think your child is able to ignore them? If your child was trying to complete an assignment, don't you think a classmate walking around will make it a bit more challenging for your child to focus? By the end of the school year, your child has lost days of academic instruction. Before I continue, give that a minute to sink in. How do you feel right about now? Are you angry? Do you want the school to do something about it?

If you answered yes, then you may be disappointed. Schools today cannot do much about this situation. Teachers can talk to students, send them to the office, or possibly suspend the student if the behaviors are serious.

Schools and teachers need help from you, the parents. This behavior, at any age, should not be accepted by parents. Now, the question you should ask yourself as a parent is, "How can I help?" First, be the authority figure and make sure your child knows very well there are home consequences. Second, please consider how this may help or hinder your child.

Pretend you are John's parent. You tell John he can walk around the room anytime he wants to and does not have to listen to his teacher. Guess what? John's teacher is practice for John's boss. Do you think John's boss is going to allow blatant disrespect and incomplete projects? I'm thinking not. John needs you to set boundaries, to explain this behavior is not acceptable at all. You can do this in a loving and kind way; however, if John needs you to be tough, then you may have to stand tall and be the adult authority figure John needs you to be. In the end, John will learn how to behave in school and in life. Side note here: I am referring to John as a typically developing child without any type of disability that may cause reason for these behaviors. Students with special needs are a different category and different situation.

Chances are if John is exhibiting these behaviors in the classroom, he is also doing these things at home. How do you think he is going to stop if you do nothing and look the other way? Do you think John will make it to college or even complete high school? How will John take care of himself and earn an honest living? You are not helping John when you ignore or put up with negative behaviors. You are hurting both John and yourself. To be completely honest, if John has siblings, they are the true victims. Who do you think John bothers the most when he is not at school pulling the hair of his classmates? Your other children, that's who. What are you going to tell them when they are adults and ask you why or how come you didn't protect them? Can you live with that? I certainly hope not.

CHAPTER 7

Message to Teachers

The first thing I would like to say here is that you are appreciated. I know, sometimes, it may not feel or look that way, but you are. I can guarantee you have made a difference to someone—most likely many little someones—and right now, there is someone who needs you desperately whether you realize it or not. Teachers, we are in the unique position of knowing exactly what a parent-teacher conference looks like from both angles. Let's use that to our advantage.

I think what most teachers would like parents to know is that teaching is stressful. When disrespect comes from students, parents, and administration, it can be tough to figure out who is on the side of the teacher. Where can the teacher go for support? Even when it feels as though everyone is against us, we are still the professionals and must conduct ourselves in that manner.

Starting a parent conference on a bad note and continuing with this methodology will not foster positive bonds between teacher and parent. I believe most teachers realize that; however, there are times when the stress takes this logic out of our brains. I am here to remind you. Kindness is never a bad thing, even when it is not reciprocated.

Start off your conference, phone call, or meeting with a smile and explain how you, as the teacher, help your student and how you are going to continue to help your student. Then follow through with communication on the outcome. Please do not lie to a parent. Do not tell them you are doing things to help their child when you are not just to appear as though you are an effective and caring teacher. Your student is the victim in this charade. Honesty really is the best policy here. If you recall, I suggested the same for parents.

For the teachers who are also parents, think back to the last time you were on the parent side of a parent-teacher conference. How did your child's teacher approach the situation, and how did it make you feel?

Of course, just because a parent is also a teacher, doesn't mean their kids will never struggle in school. They may, however, be better prepared to handle those struggles given their teaching experiences.

Now think about that parent-teacher conference. How do you think your child's teacher cares for your child? Did your child's teacher use kind words or praise or reflect on your child's growth. I would hope so. However, if they didn't, you've learned a lesson about what not to do to the parents of your current and future students. This lesson is just as valuable as any other.

Teachers, parents do appreciate you even if they do not always show it. Speaking from personal experience with parents, their supposed uncooperativeness is simply due to ignorance or frustration. For example, a parent who is struggling with a defiant child does not want to hear only about the poor choices or bad decisions their child made. I am sure you can find something kind to say about your student before you begin to mention your concerns. Focus on their intelligence, kindness, or great verbal skills. All these things combine together to create the child in your class. Consider this: How can your words foster the student and help this individual find the path to success? I can say with certainty that I may not have the answer for you right now, but I do know it is not by discussing only poor life choices of the student.

It is also a good idea to call parents just to give positive feedback. When I was in the classroom, I consistently called parents just to give them a positive update. For the students who had a history of being impulsive or having bad judgment, this was a huge step in building communication and a relationship with the parent. Often when I would call from the school phone number, the parent would hold their breath just waiting for the bad news, and often they would breathe a sigh of relief when I had nothing but good things to say.

Let's go back to our unique situation. How would you feel if your child's teachers called for something good? How would you feel if they called only for the negative? I hope this discussion at least gave you food for thought because I know teaching is challenging and rewarding. Many parents have said, with no qualms, that they would never be able to teach or work in a school. They appreciate the hard work teachers put in and value the fact that their children have quality teachers. So teachers, please remember that.

Much of the same lessons we instill in our students would work in our lives. Respect each other—that means students, parents, and colleagues. Here is a small list of important items I like to focus on.

TIP #1: RESPECT YOUR STUDENTS.

I cannot stress this enough. Students are people, too, and deserve our respect. This means everyone from kindergarten all the way up to the highest grade. Depending on where you teach, this may be fifth grade, eighth grade, or even adults at the college level. Students should be listened to, given an opportunity to explain themselves, and able to speak their feelings in a respectful tone while you listen calmly.

Often, how the parents feel about a teacher is based on what their child tells them. Please remember here that, depending on the age of the student, as mentioned before, students may not be able to explain the entire story or situation, but they will be able to provide at least some context. So teachers, please do not dismiss your students' feelings without hearing them out fully. Make sure to investigate or get someone at your school who will investigate before you decide something is unimportant. It may seem silly to you at the moment, but it isn't to the student. This may be the beginning of a relationship moving forward or sliding downhill. You are the professional. What would you want the teacher to do if the student was your child?

Have you heard the phrase to lead by example? This phrase can refer to actions, certainly, but it can also refer to words. By speaking to students, all students, with respect even when you feel like you are about to explode, you set the tone for a mutual feeling of respect. Some students may not be spoken to kindly or gently at home. While this scenario is unfortunate for the student, they may not realize there are other ways to speak to people. Their lack of knowledge can be compounded exponentially when the student is upset, frustrated, or struggling. By speaking with respect, you show the students that even when you are upset for any reason, getting angry and taking it out on others is not healthy and not an acceptable strategy.

Treating people with respect is also surprisingly good for your health, heart, and soul. I am generally a quiet and calm person. I almost never get angry and raise my voice. When another person begins to get angry and yell, I can honestly ask said individual if they can tell me how I speak to them. Usually, they say I am kind and do not scream at them. This often leads to a lowering of voices and a calm conversation that actually leads to a solution of sorts. Sometimes it is an easy fix, while other times we agree to disagree. I have realized in life there is not one person who will agree with you 100 percent of the time. While others will support you regardless due to their love for you, it is not always due to agreement. You can begin the healing process. You can be the difference between a peaceful and positive relationship rather than a combative one. I am not sure about you, but I would choose peace over arguing any day.

TIP #2: YOUR CO-TEACHERS CAN BE GREAT RESOURCES.

This can be true whether this is your first year teaching or if you can hear the retirement paperwork calling your name. Everyone has something to share. New teachers lack the experience and may need some classroom management guidance or help with lesson planning. However, veteran teachers may not be familiar or up-to-date with the latest teaching techniques, research, or ideas. Gone are the days of teachers in their classrooms spending their instructional time alone with their students. Today, most teachers share students and interacting is in everyone's best interest.

Please do not forget students have eyes also. What do I mean? Well, when a teacher is rude, gets angry, or puts another teacher or staff member down, students can see that. They can hear it, too, so if you are going to be disrespectful to a peer at school, please be sure the students are out of earshot. Or better yet, why don't you try to work things out in private? Everyone disagrees with a coworker, and schools are not any different. Teaching is stressful, undoubtedly. Did I not mention that yet? Teachers make sure all students are learning and doing their best, monitor their students' progress, meet with parents and administrators, and have so much else to do; it is not a walk in the park to be a teacher. But you are a teacher. You are in school, and you are spending your days doing all those things I just mentioned. Why not do it with grace?

More and more students with special needs have been appearing in general education classrooms. A half century ago, these students may have been taught in a closet or basement. Not anymore. Today, the voices of those with special needs are heard and, in most cases, they receive a comparable education to their neurotypical and non-disabled peers. This is a wonderful thing, but how does this connect with my message to teachers? Special education teachers have an equally stressful position. I have always said, "While the stressors may look different, they weigh the same on the shoulders of someone who cares." Someone who chose to work with students with disabilities.

Imagine you began your day not in your own classroom or your own space but in someone else's. That may stress you out just a little bit. Now, imagine that space belongs to someone who does not agree with you, does not understand you, or expects something of you that is unrealistic. How does your day begin then? I would venture to guess you start the day off worried and possibly unhappy. This is often the life of a special education teacher.

In many areas, students with disabilities are moving into the general education classrooms, where they are free to learn with everyone else, including their nondisabled peers. With this shift, the special education teacher follows along, taking her lesson plan modifications, perky personality, willingness to help, new ideas, and diverse experience with her. Of course, no one actually pays any attention to these things.

Attending to a student in someone else's classroom is not always easy, but the general education teacher has the power to help make it easier. My message here is this: For all the general education teachers who have a special education teacher in the classroom, please take a moment to put yourself in their shoes. Think about how you speak and act and welcome them into your space. If you don't think about and consider the feelings of the special education teacher, how can you start the healing process and rebuild your relationship? You need to work as a team so you don't give off any negative energy in the classroom.

I would like to add that if you do not agree with the special education teacher's style or actions, I would ask you to take the first step. Ask for a sit down where you explain this in a polite and professional manner. Give her time to respond and work out a way for the both of you to coexist for the students you share and are responsible for. Inclusion teachers, you can also ask for this. If you feel as though it is needed, chances are the other party has the same feelings. Someone needs to make the first move.

TIP #3: TREAT YOUR STUDENTS THE SAME WAY YOU WOULD TREAT YOUR CHILDREN AT HOME.
I have had many teachers tell me they treat their students as their own biological children. This does not mean they spoil or punish them; it means they give the students the same respect and boundaries. Both are needed for a healthy child-to-adult relationship.

CHAPTER 8

My Experiences
as a Parent

Sitting on the other side of the desk as the parent for a parent-teacher conference can be weird sometimes. It's almost the same feeling as when you accidentally put your sock on inside out and can feel the seams. That kind of weird. But we love our own children just as much as our students and make sure to attend as caring parents. Well, most of us do. That does nothing to say this meeting will always go smoothly or that we instantly have a connection because we bond as teachers. Most of the time, something like that does occur. I like to refer to it as "professional courtesy." But sometimes, there is no such thing as professional courtesy, and the gloves come off.

Here is a particularly negative experience I wish never would have occurred.

I was once told at the beginning of a parent-teacher conference nine weeks into the year that my child could not control himself and talked constantly. The teacher continued on this path, stating that my child would be retained due to this behavior. At the time, I thought to myself, *Hmm, would talking be cause for retention?* Possibly, if it was a symptom of an underlying, more serious situation or concern. In that case, yes, we should talk about retention. However, if the student was just acting immaturely, then that was where I came in, the parent.

I asked the teacher why they hadn't contacted me even once in the nine weeks if this was such a problem. They had my phone number and email address, and I worked about a mile away in another school in the same district, which they were well aware of. Had the teacher handled our interaction in the best manner? Absolutely not!

Now, have I done things wrong in parent-teacher conferences? Yes, I am sure of it. I am definitely not a perfect saint.

I then started to think about it from the other's perspective. I put myself in the teacher's shoes. In the teacher's defense, we all have bad days and then there are really bad days. Perhaps her impulsive statement about retention was the outcome of the stress of the profession. I could move on and so could the teacher. We found a way to move forward for the sake of the student in question, in this particular case, my child. It turns out his behavior really wasn't that bad, and the teacher was feeling the pressure from other sources, such as the school administration and county office, and therefore lashed out at me with the threat of retention. While I am sorry this situation happened to me, I am also thankful that it did. Why, you ask? Well, that is simple. If it happened to me, that means it did not happen to a young, single parent who may not have known how to handle the situation or to a parent of a child with a disability. Thankfully, it didn't.

What I learned from this particular scenario was how to come to a mutual understanding with another adult who is meaningful to my child even when I may not agree with their thoughts or actions. It gave me insight into how some parents may have felt when they did not agree with the classroom teacher. As the special education teacher, I was often the monkey in the middle, trying to find a solution for both general education teacher and parent that satisfied everyone equally. In some situations, I have had parents ask me if their child would be singled out or mistreated by the adults in the building because the teacher was upset with the parent. I knew, without a doubt, this fear, while legitimate, would never occur. Now I say that because, in my experience, it has never occurred, and I have yet to meet a teacher who is mean to a child due to the dislike of a parent. This does not mean it has never occurred or will never occur. I simply do not have any experience with such a situation, and I am thankful for that.

Now that the negative experience has been explained, let's discuss the positive conferences I have had. These, by far, outrank the number of negative experiences. In fact, I can count on just one hand how many times a parent-teacher conference has not gone well. I am hoping to keep this number on one hand for the entirety of my children's educational years. I still have to get through the high school years, but I am feeling lucky.

I can recall one parent-teacher conference vividly. I was greeted by the teacher with a smile, and the first thing out of her mouth was something positive. She had work samples to display as well. So far so good, right? Teachers, how is she doing? We then proceeded to discuss some of the things that could be improved. Now this does not mean there was a problem. For all the nonteacher parents, all humans have the capacity to grow, improve, and evolve to become better versions of ourselves. I continue to do this daily, even well into adulthood. Are you intellectually and emotionally the same person you were a year ago? Five years ago? Possibly longer? Simply because a teacher has ideas about what your child can do better does not mean, in any way, your child is wrong or there is a problem. We do not want our students to keep moving forward without any ambition or purpose, even if they are stellar at academics, manners, and anything else. We encourage growth. These suggestions are meant to help your child, not demean them or single out their faults. Please consider this rationale next time you are sitting in a parent-teacher conference.

Teachers, the parents of your students likely know you have a classroom of students. They may even be aware of the exact number of classmates their child has. It does no good to begin the conference with informing the parent of how many other children are in your care. Think of it this way. You show up to the doctor's office and are promptly informed you must wait to be seen, as your doctor is currently caring for others. Do you feel like a priority when you finally make it back after all the waiting, only for your doctor to begin with a statement of how exhausted they are due to the many patients they've already seen for the day? Would you trust this individual with your health? No! Education is just as important. Teachers, when you have a conference with a parent, they are present for their child. These parents are giving you time and attention to discuss their child. The last thing they want to hear is how many other students are causing you stress.

CHAPTER 9

My Experiences as a Teacher

'll start from the beginning here. It's not when I received my first paycheck or my first classroom. For teachers, the job begins with student teaching. Let me start this chapter with my student teaching experience. It was at a high school in New York City. My bachelor's degree was in history. My teaching license that I was working toward at the time was secondary education social studies. In the state of New York, that meant grades seven through twelve. I had two classes to teach. One was American History, grade eleven, and the second was World History, grade nine. I had one mentor per class. One mentor was an older gentleman getting close to retirement while the other was a young woman just a few years older than me. The experiences could not have been more different.

I can still remember everything perfectly. I had a classroom of about fifty students. Yes, I will wait for your brain to take a look at that number again. Fifty. I did not have that many the first day of the semester, but as the days passed and students needed the class, they were put in. Numbers meant nothing it seemed. New York City is full of people and is very crowded. I know—you are shocked! How does the city that never sleeps, the Empire State, pack so many people into such a small area? All I can say is the population is very dense, and there are many New York City public schools with the same concern. It was so bad, the high school had two different start and end times. The students who began their day at 7:15 a.m. ended classes by 1:00 p.m. The students who started later in the day were there until 4:00 p.m.

Just some food for thought. Have you seen a high schooler at 7:00 a.m.? What do you think they look like? Did you say half of the them are asleep on their desks? Yup, that would be correct. What? You said half the students missed the bus or train and didn't even show up until the end of class? You must be a genius or psychic because you are correct once again. There were very few students who were there and ready to learn, but that is for another time and another day. Today, we are focused on student teaching and this particular experience.

Eventually, I had more bodies than chairs and desks in the room. Students sat on window ledges or stood. I almost decided teaching was not the career for me. Then I realized, if I did that, I was part of the problem and not the solution. The solution is whatever is best for the students, any age and every stage. So I stayed, and almost twenty years later, I am struggling to find a way to be part of the solution. Hopefully, this book will bring awareness. Maybe my voice will be the loudest. Students need more than what we are giving them in this country.

Back to my student teaching experience. Buckle up, it's going to be a bumpy ride.

I went to meet my mentor prior to the start of my student teaching. He was strong-minded and did not let me really get a word in edgewise. He was very experienced and ... I think disgruntled would be the best word that fits his description. To look at him, he was tall and thin with just a whisper of a beard. He wore jeans and a pair of old sneakers. In his defense, he did have on a shirt with a collar and three buttons; it was a polo-style shirt. He did not look at my lesson plans at all. I felt hurt at the time; after putting in so much work and thought, he did not even care enough to fake interest. It had seemed that the profession, or perhaps other aspects of his life, had sucked him dry, and he simply did not have any more to give. At my age now, I can understand how life can beat someone up; however, twenty-year-old me was bright-eyed and ready to take on the world. My eyes then saw something completely different.

My mentor proceeded to introduce me to the class on the first day. He then shocked the life out of me.

He sat down on his chair, which looked like a perfect fit for a public school with not enough funding. It was old and wiggled and looked thin and sad. He then continued on his quest to relax. He put his feet up on the desk and opened up his newspaper, a newspaper that opened up as long and wide as *The New York Times,* thus hiding his face from me as well as the students who were only a few years younger than I was. This was the routine each day for the period.

Did I mention I was shy? Yes, I was and still am painfully shy, and it is awful. I probably have a disorder. I have worked to overcome my debilitating bashfulness, but it is a challenge every day. Now you know my dirty little secret. So, now that we have that established, the answer to your question of how I allowed this to continue is hopefully answered. If not, maybe more information will shed some light.

I was also a naïve young person, and combined with being way too shy, I could not bear to even say anything to him, so I agreed and followed his lead. I never reported his attitude or asked a professor for help. I was afraid he would get in trouble and then I would get in trouble. The possibility that he would even accuse me of lying went through my head, and then I would have to prove I was telling the truth. *Who would believe me?* I thought. I wish I would have had the confidence to say something. Maybe I would have had a more positive experience and maybe those fifty students would have as well. Perhaps nothing would have been accomplished. I guess I'll never know. It is a regret I have to live with. I now find comfort in knowing I am conscious and aware of those around me. I try to make sure those working under me are comfortable and secure. I do not, of course, give this person any credit for helping me learn how to teach. I treat my students and co-teachers with respect because I feel it is the right thing to do.

My other mentor was a much different person. She took the time to sit with me and treat me as one of the teachers. I sat with her during her planning; she looked at my lesson plans, and she actually gave me great advice. While she was always a professional, she never said a negative word about my other mentor. She did not say a word when I asked her for advice and support for his classroom and students.

The positive interaction was exactly what I needed to stay in the profession, but I viewed both experiences as learning opportunities. It was then I saw teachers through the eyes of an adult and not a child or a student. I saw some put in more effort and care while others were simply in it for the paycheck (not that it's much). An unhappy teacher can wreak havoc in ways I now realize. The ripple effect is dangerous. That brings us full circle to the reason for this book.

Parents and teachers need to work together for the benefit of the student, for the future of individuals, and for this country we all love so dearly. If everyone does the right thing, maybe we can make some progress and grow. This is what I took with me as I entered the workforce as a licensed teacher.

Student teaching has now come to an end. While it was free labor for the city of New York, it gave me a purpose and a reason to get up in the morning. Okay, Christina, time to get serious, I would tell myself. Time to get a teaching job and start my career. Easier said than done, I quickly learned. It seemed like every school wanted teachers with experience or who spoke Spanish. I had neither under my belt or on my resume.

The question that stood before me was this: How was I ever going to get experience if everyone only wants experienced teachers? While deep into my job search, my husband joined the United States Army and off we moved to North Carolina.

Spoiler alert: culture shock!

Going from New York City to a small North Carolina town was not anything I would have ever been able to explain in words. I can still remember when I was new to the state, standing in line at a gas station holding my young son. He was about one year old. The man in front of me—he looked about sixty and I was twenty-five—turned around and commented on the weather. In my head, I tried to determine if he was flirting with me or distracting me so he could steal my wallet. After all, in New York (at that time), people did not just simply make conversation with strangers in a line. They talked to people they wanted to date or rob. And I had to get over that mindset if I was going to work in North Carolina schools.

I was able to get a job rather quickly as a teacher of adult learners while I put in the paperwork to move my teaching license from New York to North Carolina. Secondary-level history positions were hard to come by, and I was unable to secure a full-time position in the first year. In my mind, I had always regretted getting my teaching license in the field of special education. To me, my inability to land the job I desired was a sign, I ended up getting a master's degree in special education. I knew I had found my calling. My heart is with students with disabilities. I cannot see my life outside this field in any manner.

When you invest in teachers, you invest in your children. Investing in your children is ensuring the future of the United States of America.

Conclusion

I hope both parents and teachers take to heart some of my suggestions and experiences. Everything written on the pages is meant to help bridge the gap in communication between teachers and parents as well as share information. In an ever-changing world where everyone over the age of eight has a camera to take pictures or videos, various social media accounts, and essentially limitless access to the internet, we live life differently than even a decade ago. In many ways, navigating life is even more challenging.

I want to make it a little easier for teachers and parents to work together. To do so, I am asking both parents and teachers to consider what's so special about the other. What I mean is this: Parents, tell me who your favorite teacher is and why. Teachers, who is your most supportive parent? Once you have thought of someone, please go to my website **www.ourchildsfuture.com** and complete the short survey. There is a link available that will allow you to brag about the fabulous parent or teacher of your choice. The survey allows you to leave your contact information. However, doing so is completely optional.

I hope to hear from you soon!

Endnotes

1 Sutcher, Darling-Hammond, and Carver-Thomas, *A Coming Crisis,* chap. 5.

2 ———, *A Coming Crisis,* executive summary; ———, *A Coming Crisis,* chap. 1; ———, *A Coming Crisis,* chap. 5.

3 ———, *A Coming Crisis,* chap. 5.

4 ———, *A Coming Crisis,* chap. 1.

5 Cleary, "The Number One Factor."

6 Sutcher, Darling-Hammond, and Carver-Thomas, *A Coming Crisis,* chap. 5.

7 ———, *A Coming Crisis,* executive summary; ———, *A Coming Crisis,* chap. 1; ———, *A Coming Crisis,* chap. 3.

8 ———, *A Coming Crisis,* introduction.

9 ———, *A Coming Crisis,* executive summary.

10 ———, *A Coming Crisis,* executive summary; ———, *A Coming Crisis,* chap. 2.

11 Banks, "Foods for children,"; U.S. Department of Health and Human Services and U.S. Department of Agriculture, *2015–2020 Dietary Guidelines,* executive summary.

12 ———, *2015–2020 Dietary Guidelines,* executive summary; ———, *2015–2020 Dietary Guidelines,* introduction; ———, *2015–2020 Dietary Guidelines,* chap. 1.

13 DiSalvo, "Too Much Sugar."

14 ———, "Too Much Sugar."

15 Harvard Health Publishing, "Foods linked."

16 ———, "Foods linked."

17 ———, "Foods linked"; U.S. Department of Health and Human Services and U.S. Department of Agriculture, *2015–2020 Dietary Guidelines,* chap. 1.

18 DiSalvo, "Too Much Sugar."

19 ———, "Too Much Sugar"; Harvard Health Publishing, "Foods linked."

20 Mayo Clinic, "Added sugars."

21 U.S. Department of Health and Human Services and U.S. Department of Agriculture, *2015–2020 Dietary Guidelines,* executive summary; ———, *2015–2020 Dietary Guidelines,* introduction; ———, *2015–2020 Dietary Guidelines,* chap. 1.

22 Mayo Clinic, "Added sugars."

23 DiSalvo, "Too Much Sugar."

Bibliography

Aldeman, Chad. "How Many Teachers Retire Each Year?"
Teacher Pensions Blog. June 19, 2015. https://www.
teacherpensions.org/blog/how-many-teachers-retire-each-year.

Banks, Jacqueline Silvestri. "Foods for children with autism."
Fox News. Updated October 24, 2015.

Cleary, Jennifer. "The Number One Factor in Student Success?
Relationships with Teachers." *Core Instruction* (blog).
Education Week Teacher. October 24, 2018. https://www.
learningsciences.com/blog/number-1-factor/.

DiSalvo, David. "What Eating Too Much Sugar Does to
Your Brain." April 27, 2012. *Psychology Today*. https://www.
psychologytoday.com/us/blog/neuronarrative/201204/what-
eating-too-much-sugar-does-your-brain.

Harvard Health Publishing. "Foods linked to better
brainpower." Healthbeat. https://www.health.harvard.edu/
mind-and-mood/foods-linked-to-better-brainpower.

Mayo Clinic. "Added sugars: Don't get sabotaged by sweeteners." Healthy Lifestyle. January 30, 2019. https://www.mayoclinic.org/healthy-lifestyle/nutrition-and-healthy-eating/in-depth/added-sugar/art-20045328.

Sutcher, Leib, Linda Darling-Hammond, and Desiree Carver-Thomas. *A Coming Crisis in Teaching?: Teacher Supply, Demand, and Shortages in the U.S.* Palo Alto, CA: Learning Policy Institute, 2016. https://learningpolicyinstitute.org/sites/default/files/productfiles/A_Coming_Crisis_in_Teaching_REPORT.pdf.

U.S. Department of Health and Human Services and U.S. Department of Agriculture. *2015–2020 Dietary Guidelines for Americans.* 8th ed. Washington D.C., USDA, 2015. https://health.gov/sites/default/files/2019-09/2015-2020_Dietary_Guidelines.pdf.